the devil's cup

STEWART LEE ALLEN

CANONGATE

First published in the United States of America
in 1999 by Soho Press Inc., New York

Published in Great Britain in 2000 by
Canongate Books Ltd, 14 High Street,
Edinburgh EH1 1TE

This paperback edition first published in 2001

Reprinted in 2002

10 9 8 7 6 5 4 3

British Library Cataloguing-in-Publication Data
A catalogue record for this book is available on
request from the British Library

ISBN 1 84195 143 9

Book design by James Reyman Studio
Printed and bound by Omnia Books Ltd, Glasgow

www.canongate.net

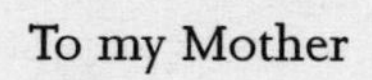
To my Mother

Contents

Introduction

the First Cup

As with art 'tis prepared,
so you should drink it with art.
Abd el Kader (sixteenth century)

Nairobi, Kenya
1988

"ETHIOPIA IS THE BEST." BILL'S EYES BRIGHTENED. "FINEST GRUB in Africa, mate. And those Ethiopian girls..."

"No girls," I said. Bill, a Cockney plumber/Buddhist monk, was obsessed with finding me a girl but lacked discretion; his last bit of matchmaking had ended with me fending off a Kenyan hooker, twice my size, who'd kept shouting, "I am just ready for love!"

"No girls," I repeated, shuddering at the memory. "Don't even think about it."

"You don't have to bonk them." He gave me his most charming leer. "But you'll want to."

"I sincerely doubt it."

"And the *buna*, ahhh! Best *buna* in the world."

"*Buna*? What's that?"

"Coffee," he said. "Ethiopia's where it came from."

So it was settled. We were off to Ethiopia for lunch. Buses are rare here in northern Kenya, so we hitched a ride in the back of a rickety "Tata" truck loaded with soda pop. It was a desolate trip, twenty hours of sun-blackened rock and pale weeds. The main indication of human habitation was the machine-gun-riddled buses abandoned on the roadside. We were not particularly worried about bandits (there were two armed guards on our vehicle), but about seven hours into the trip we passed a truck whose offer of a ride we had earlier declined. Its axle had been snapped in two by the unpaved road, flipping the vehicle over and killing the driver and half the passengers. Those who had survived, all seven-foot-tall Masai warriors, with traditional red robes and elongated earlobes, were standing about weeping, and shaking their spears at the sky. One of the Masai lay crushed to death under a pile of shattered Pepsi bottles.

When we arrived at Ethiopia, the border was closed. The sole guard was friendly but adamant—no foreigners allowed into Ethiopia. Bill clarified our position. We didn't want to go into Ethiopia, he explained. We only wanted to visit the village of Moyale, half of which just happened to *be* in Ethiopia. Surely, Bill reasoned, that was allowed?

The guard considered. It was true, he said, foreigners were allowed to visit Moyale for the day. Then he wagged his head: but not on Sunday. Ethiopia, he reminded us, is a Christian nation.

Bill tried another approach. Was there an Ethiopian Tourist Guesthouse in Moyale? he asked. Of course, said the soldier. Did we wish to visit it?

"*Owwww*," said Bill, giving the Ethiopian language's breathy affirmative.

"No problem," said the guard. "Go straight ahead and just left."

The government hotels are always overpriced, so we located a local restaurant—a shack, to be exact, with dirt floors and a dry grass roof. The food was excellent: *doro wat* (spicy chicken stew with rancid butter), *injera* (fermented crepes), and *tej* (honey mead). Then came coffee.

Ethiopians were drinking coffee while Europeans were still taking beer for breakfast, and over the centuries a ceremony has developed around sharing the brew. First, green beans are roasted at the table. The hostess then passes the still-smoking beans around so each guest may fully enjoy the aroma. A quasi-blessing or ode to friendship is offered, and the beans are ground in a stone mortar, then brewed.

That was how the restaurant owner prepared our coffee that day and, while I've had it performed many times since, never has it seemed so lovely. She was a typical Ethiopian country woman, tall, elegant, and stunningly beautiful, wearing orange and violet wraps that glowed in the darkened hut. And the coffee, served in handleless demitasses with a fresh sprig of ginger-like herb, was excellent.

In the full-fledged ceremony, which can last up to an hour, you must take three cups: *Abole-Berke-Sostga*, one-two-three, for friendship. Unfortunately, our hostess had only enough beans for one cup each. Come back tomorrow, she said, there will be more. Evening curfew was approaching, so we hurried back to the Kenyan side of the border. The next day, however, the guards refused to let us back into Ethiopia. We stood arguing at the border for hours, but nothing, neither reasoning nor bribes, convinced them to let us back in for that promised second cup.

During the next ten years Ethiopia fell to pieces. Millions died in famines, civil war broke out, and eventually the country split in two. My life was hardly better run. I lived on four continents and in eleven cities, sometimes moving five times in a single year. The only thing that made it bearable was the knowledge that at the age of thirty-five I would drop everything and return to the road—"go for a walk," as I was fond of saying, never to return. Consider it a passive-aggressive death wish. If I were a wannabe Buddhist, I could have claimed it was a desire for "Loss of Self." Whatever. Instead, I accidentally fell in love (another type of death wish) and headed to Australia to get married, an ill-fated scheme that, by means too complicated to explain, ended with me working at Mother Theresa's Calcutta hospice for the dying.

Calcutta is the world's greatest city, and I'll tell you why: unendurable suffering, arrogance, benevolence, intelligence, and greed thrive side-by-side, face-to-face, twenty-four hours a day, with no apology. On one bus ride I watched a woman fall dead of starvation, while across the street children in immaculate white school uniforms shrieked with pleasure over a game of croquet; two blocks earlier I'd seen a woman immersed up to her neck in a muddy pond, intently praying to the sun.

It's also a bibliophile's delight, and it was here, while prowling the city's innumerable bookstalls, that I discovered a curious manuscript. The print was almost illegible, and the prose the quaintly archaic, singsong English of the subcontinent. I have no idea what it was called, since the cover had long ago rotted off. I suppose it was typical stuff, just another half-crazed Hindi rant about how dietary imbalances in the West were creating a race of hyperactive sociopaths hell-bent on destroying Mother Earth. Most of the tract kvetched about meat eaters (Hindus are vegetarians) and cow killers (Holy Beast, that). But the section that caught my eye was the one lamenting the evils of "that dark and evil bean from Africa." I paraphrase:

> *Is it any wonder, I ask the reader, that it is told how the black-skinned savages of that continent eat the coffee bean before sacrificing living victims to their gods? One need only compare the violent coffee-drinking societies of the West to the peace-loving tea drinkers of the Orient to realize the pernicious and malignant effect that bitter brew has upon the human soul.*

You-are-what-you-eat fruitcakes are as common in India as in California. But what struck me was the contrast to an eighteenth-century French book I'd happened upon in Hanoi, Vietnam. The book, *Mon Journal*, was written by social critic and historian Jules Michelet, and in it he essentially attributes the birth of an enlightened Western civilization to Europe's transformation into a coffee-drinking society: "For this sparkling outburst of creative thought there is no doubt that the honor should be ascribed in part to the great event which created new customs and even changed the human temperament—the advent of coffee."

How French, I'd thought at the time, to attribute the birth of Western civilization to an espresso. But Michelet's notion is curiously similar to modern research indicating that certain foods have affected history in previously unsuspected ways. Specialists in the field, called ethnobotany, have recently theorized that eating certain mushrooms can alter brain function. Others have reported that the sacred jaguars depicted by the Mayans are actually frogs that the priests consumed en masse for their hallucinogenic properties. Recent research has indicated that the sacred violet of the pharaohs was considered holy because of its intoxicating powers. These foods are all drugs, of course.

But so is coffee—as an addict, I should know. Perhaps Michelet had been on to something. When had Europeans started drinking coffee, and what had it replaced? I was clueless. I Certainly had no idea that finding the answer would take me three quarters of the way around the world, roughly twenty thousand miles, by train, dhow, rickshaw, cargo freighter, and, finally, a donkey. Even now, penning this page, I don't know what to make of what I've written. At times, it seems like the ramblings of a hypercaffeinated hophead; at others, a completely credible study. All I knew in Calcutta was that the logical place to start looking for confirmation of Michelet's proposition was in the land where coffee had first been discovered over two thousand years ago, the country I'd been waiting to revisit for a decade.

It was time to head to Ethiopia and get that second cup.

A Season in Hell

Abole, Berke, Sostga—one, two, three cups,
and we are friends forever.
Con artist in Addis Ababa

Harrar, Ethiopia

"YOU LIKE RAM-BO?"

My questioner was a wiry Arab-African squatting in the shade of a white clay wall. Sharp eyes, wispy mustache, white turban. Not your typical Sylvester Stallone fan.

"Rambo?" I repeated uncertainly.

He nodded. "Ram-bo." He adjusted his filthy wraparound so the hem didn't drag in the dirt. "Ram-bo," he repeated with infinite disinterest. "*Farangi*."

"Are you really a Rambo fan?" I was surprised—Charles

Bronson had been more popular in Calcutta. I flexed my biceps to clarify. "You like?"

The man looked at me in disgust. "Ram-bo," he insisted. "Ram-*boo*, Ram-*boooo*. You go? You like?"

"No go," I said, walking off. "No like."

I'd just arrived in Harrar, a remote village in the Ethiopian highlands, after a grueling twenty-four hour train journey from the capital, Addis Ababa. I already preferred Harrar. Its winding alleys were free of both cars and thieves, a big improvement over Addis, where pickpockets followed me like flies and my one night out had ended in an attempted robbery after a "friendship coffee ceremony." I also liked Harrar's Arabic flavor, the whitewashed mud buildings, and the colorful gypsy-African clothes worn by the girls. Rambo Man had been the only hustler so far, and he seemed reasonable enough.

I found a suitable café and grabbed a table in the shade. The coffee, brewed on an old handpulled espresso machine, was a thick black liquor served in a shot glass. The taste was shocking in the intensity of its "coffeeness," a trait I attributed to minor burns incurred in the pan-roasting technique common in Ethiopia. Harrarian coffee beans are among the world's finest, second only to Jamaican and Yemeni, but this... I suspected local beans had been mixed with smuggled Zairean Robusta, which would account for the fine head of *crema* (called *wesh* here), as well as the fact that after one cup I felt like crawling out of my skin.

I ordered a second. Rambo Man had come to stare at me from across the road. Our eyes met. He shrugged his shoulders and raised his hands suggestively. I scowled.

Harrar is one of the legendary cities of African antiquity. It was closed to foreigners for centuries because an Islamic saint had prophesied its fall the day a non-Muslim entered the walls. Christians who attempted to enter were beheaded; African merchants were merely locked outside and left to the tender mercies of local lion packs. Not that inside was much better. Hyenas roamed the streets, noshing on the homeless. Witchcraft and slavery flourished, particularly the notorious selling of black eunuchs to Turkish harems. By the 1800s, the walled city had become so isolated that a separate language had developed. It is still spoken today.

This reputation drew Europe's most intrepid adventurers to Harrar. Many tried, many died, until Sir Richard Burton, the Englishman who "discovered" the source of the Nile, managed to enter the city in 1855 disguised as an Arab. It fell soon afterward.

The most intriguing of Harrar's early Western visitors, however, was the French Symbolist poet Arthur Rimbaud. Rimbaud had come to Paris when he was seventeen. After a year of pursuing his famous "derangement of the senses" lifestyle, he'd established a reputation as the most depraved man in the city. By nineteen, he'd finished his masterpiece, *A Season in Hell*. Having reached his twentieth year, he renounced all poetry and disappeared off the face of the earth. Rimbaud...

"*Rambo!*" I shouted, jumping out of my chair. That's what the fellow had been going on about—Rimbaud, pronounced "Rambo." He'd wanted to take me to Rimbaud's mansion. The poet had not "disappeared off the face of the earth" when he'd abandoned poetry in 1870. He'd merely come to his senses and become a coffee merchant in Harrar.

Rambo Man, however, had vanished.

Rimbaud's reason for coming to Ethiopia was more complicated than a desire to enter the coffee trade. He was actually fulfilling a passage from *A Season in Hell*, in which he predicted going to a land "of lost climates" from which he would return "with limbs of iron, bronzed skin, and fierce eyes." He wanted action, danger, and money. He got at least the first two in Harrar.

The emir had been deposed only twenty years earlier, and tensions were still high. The French coffee merchants needed someone crazy enough to risk his life for a bean (albeit one going for one hundred dollars a pound). Rimbaud was their man.

The importance of the Harrar Longberry, however, goes beyond the fragrant cup it produces. Many believe it is here that the lowly Robusta bean evolved into the civilized Arabica, potentially making the Harrar Longberry the missing link of the genus *Coffea*. To understand the importance of this you must first know that there are two basic species of coffee beans: the luscious Arabica from East Africa, which prefers higher elevations, and the reviled Robusta from Zaire, which grows just about anywhere.

That being understood, we must now go back to that mysterious time before the dawn of civilization, the Precaffeinated Era.

Back then, fifteen hundred to three thousand years ago, the world's first coffee lovers, the nomadic Oromos, lived in the kingdom of Kefa.[1] The Oromos didn't actually drink coffee; they ate it, crushed, mixed with fat, and shaped into golf-ball-size treats. They were especially fond of munching on these coffee-balls before going into battle against the people of Bonga, who generally beat the pants off the Oromos. The Bongas also happened to be first-rate slave traders, and sent about seven thousand slaves each year to the Arabic markets in Harrar. A fair number of these unfortunates were Oromos coffee chewers who had been captured in battle. It was these people who accidentally first brought the bean to Harrar. Ethiopian

---

[1] *Kefa*, some say, is the root for the word *coffee*. More contend that coffee derives from the Arabic *qahwa*, from the root *q-h-w-y*, "to "make something repugnant." *Qahwa* originally referred to wine, which made food repugnant, and was applied to coffee because it made sleep repugnant. It's interesting to note that Ethiopia is the only country in the world that does not use a word similar to *coffee* for the brew; there, it's called *buna*, which means bean.

The Kefans also gave us the world's first baristas, a caste called the Tofaco, who not only brewed the king's coffee but also poured it down his throat.

rangers say the old slave trails are still shaded by the coffee trees that have grown from their discarded meals.

But the important thing is the difference between the regions' plants. Beans from relatively low-lying Kefa grow in huge coffee jungles and are generally more akin to the squat, harsh Robustas that probably came out of the jungles of Zaire thousands of years before. Harrar's beans, by contrast, are long-bodied and possess delicious personalities like the Arabicas. In adapting to Harrar's higher altitude, something wonderful seems to have happened to them. No one knows what, but we should all be grateful that it was the evolved Arabica beans of Harrar that were later brought to Yemen, and then to the world at large.

So Rimbaud's risking his life for the bean (in fact, it killed him) is perhaps not so unreasonable. It's worth noting, however, that the poet/merchant did not seem to hold Harrar's coffee in high regard. "Horrible" is how he describes it in one letter; "awful stuff" and "disgusting." Oh well. Perhaps all those years of absinthe had dulled his taste buds. The fact that the locals were fond of selling him beans laced with goat shit probably didn't help matters.

After a few more cups, I checked into a hotel and set out in search of Rimbaud's home. Harrar is a small place of about twenty thousand inhabitants; a maze of alleys lined with lopsided mosques, mudhuts. It is noticeably lacking in street names. Rimbaud's house is probably the easiest thing to find in the city, since any foreigner who approaches is mobbed by wannabe tour guides. I had no intention of paying anybody for guiding me to a house, and eventually, by taking the most obscure route imaginable, I managed to reach what I knew was Rimbaud's neighborhood undetected, only to find myself in a dead-end alley.

There was nobody in sight, so I yelled a cautious hello.

"Here," came a familiar voice.

I crawled through a jagged crack in one of the walls, and there, squatting on a pile of rubble, was Rambo Man.

"Aha!" he shouted. "You have come at last."

He was sitting in front of one of the oddest houses I'd ever seen. At least it seemed so in the context of Harrar's one-story mud huts. It was three stories high with twin peaked gables, all covered in elaborate carvings. The shingled roof was fringed with fleur-de-lis decorations and the windows were stained red. Straight out of a Grimm's fairy tale, I thought. The oddest thing, though, was how the mansion was surrounded by a twelve-foot-high mud wall with no opening other than the crack that I'd just crawled through.

The man was looking at me in surprise. "You have no guide?"

"Guide? What for?"

"No problem." He waved a yellow piece of paper at me and demanded ten birra.

"What are these?" I asked.

"Tickets."

"Tickets? Are they real?"

"See them." He seemed vaguely offended. *Ticket—Rimbaud*, said the piece of paper. *10 Br*. "You see—real house. Government. Not like the others."

"You mean there are other Rimbaud houses?"

"No. Only one."

I paid him, and he led me up a narrow interior stairway into a huge chamber, perhaps three thousand square feet, with a fifty-foot-high ceiling ringed by an old-fashioned oval balcony. The walls were covered in handpainted canvas "wallpaper," now so filthy and tattered that I could barely make out the quaint Parisian garden scenes and heraldic devices. Huge dust particles floated about. There was no furniture of any kind.

The great French poet spent the last days of his life in this surreal château, alone except for his beloved manservant. He wrote no poetry, and his letters were filled with complaints of loneliness, disease, and his financial problems, including a disastrous attempt to sell slaves and guns to the Ethiopian emperor. His prophecy of coming home with "limbs of iron...and fierce eyes" proved false. He returned to France delirious and destitute. His left leg had been amputated. A mysterious infection soon killed him.

I wandered about for a while, peering over the balcony, touching the walls. The place seemed uninhabited. A boy in rags trailed after me only to flee as soon as I spoke. Pigeons cooed from nests among the tattered wall hangings.

As I left, the man asked me if I wanted to meet Rimbaud's descendants.

"There were daughters," he said. "Rimbaud's daughters..."

"Rimbaud had children?" I asked.

"Many daughters. Very beautiful girls...so young..." he stopped, suggestively. "You want Rambo girl?"

To sleep with the bastard offspring of Arthur Rimbaud, I thought; that would be a story. She would be beautiful, as all the women here were, and perfectly arrogant, as behooved one of Ethiopian-French descent. It was tempting. But hadn't it been a case of Harrarian clap that killed Rimbaud? I declined.

Don't roast your coffee beans in the marketplace.
(Don't tell secrets to strangers.)
Oromo nomad saying

I MET ABERA TESHONE WHILE LOOKING FOR THE HYENA MEN, a caste that feeds Harrar's trash to the packs of hyenas that gather nightly outside the city walls. The caste started as a way of keeping the animals from entering the city and attacking humans. Today it's largely a tourist attraction, although the sight of hideous animals accepting garbage from men in rags is not likely to topple the Disney empire.

Abera, a young man with a withered left leg, had been my guide for the event, and afterward we'd gone for a beer. He wanted to know why I had come to Harrar.

"Not many tourists come here," he explained.

"I noticed. I came here to learn about coffee." A thought struck me. "Hey, didn't you say you were an agriculture student? What do you know about its origin?"

"Do you know the story about Kaldi and the dancing goats?"

"Of course," I said. It's one of coffee's mythological chestnuts. It goes like this:

> *An Ethiopian goatherd named Kaldi one day noticed his best goat dancing about and baaing like a maniac. It seemed to happen after the old billy goat had been nibbling the berries off a certain plant. The goatherd tried a few himself and soon was dancing about, too.*
>
> *A holy man wandered by and asked the boy why he was dancing with a goat. The goatherd explained. The monk took some berries home and found that after eating them he could not sleep. It so happened that this holy man was famous for his rather tedious all-night sermons and was having trouble keeping his disciples awake. So he immediately ordered all his disciples, called dervishes, to chew the bean before he preached. The dervishes' sleepiness vanished, and word spread about the great prophet whose electrifying wisdom kept you awake until dawn.*

Being a city boy, I mentioned to Abera that it seemed strange that the goats would eat berries. Didn't they normally prefer leafy stuff?

"Yes, well, perhaps it was so," he said. "That is how the

country folk still make it."

"They make coffee out of leaves?"

"Yes. They call it *kati*."

"Really? I would like to try it. Maybe in a café..."

"Oh no," he laughed. "This is only drunk in the home. Hardly anyone in Harrar drinks it today. You must visit the Ogaden. They still drink it."

"Where do they live?"

"The Ogaden? They live now in Jiga-Jiga." He made the place sound like a disease. "But you can't go there. It's very, very dangerous. And those Somalis, those Ogaden, are very arrogant. So rude!"

"Why? What is the problem?

"They are rude people!" Abera shook his head angrily at the Ogaden's poor manners. "Why, just not long ago they did a bad thing to a bus going there. To all the men."

"Bad? How bad?"

"Why, very bad. They killed them."

"That's pretty bad," I agreed.

According to Abera, Ogaden bandits had pulled all the men off a bus heading to Jiga-Jiga and demanded they each recite a verse from the Koran. Those who failed were shot in the head. Thousands of the Ogaden, a desert nomad tribe, had recently been forced into refugee settlements as a result of the collapse of the Somali government. The largest camp was near Jiga-Jiga on the Ethiopian/Somali border, and as a consequence the whole area was buzzing with guerrilla activity. The recent turmoil in Mogadishu, where dead American soldiers had been dragged through the streets, had made the Ogaden especially hostile toward Yanks. The situation had grown so difficult that the relief agencies no longer sent white workers to Jiga-Jiga for fear they'd be shot.

"It is very bad for foreigners to go there," he said. "But why do you want to go?"

"I just want a cup of coffee," I said. "Have you actually been there?"

"It's Hell." Abera looked down his nose. "I urge you not to go."

IT WAS A PLEASANT TWO-HOUR DRIVE FROM HARRAR TO Jiga-Jiga, through the so-called Valley of Wonders, although what makes this valley so wondrous I couldn't say. I had set out at five in the morning, Abera having warned me that drivers refused to return from Jiga-Jiga after two in the afternoon for fear of bandits. He'd recommended I get an early start and head back to Harrar before noon unless I intended to stay overnight, in which case I'd most likely find my hotel robbed at gunpoint. That was assuming, of course, that anyone would be stupid enough to let me stay at their lodge. Was he being a tad paranoid? Perhaps. At any rate, it was a refreshingly cool way to start the day. By the time we'd reached the desert's edge, however, it had grown so warm that some of my fellow passengers removed the pistols cached beneath their shirts.

"The human head, once struck off, does not regrow like the rose." This observation was made by a British officer when Sir Richard Burton proposed visiting here in 1854, and it kept running through my head. The parallels between Burton's and my quests were starting to seem spooky. We were both seeking mysterious "bodies of water" in Central Africa; my mysterious liquid contained a few coffee beans, but other than that, we were looking for the same thing. Burton wanted to see how the Nile started out; I wanted to see how some of it ended up. Burton wound up with a Somali spear stuck through both cheeks, which is about where I hoped the parallels would cease.

Jiga-Jiga proved to be a dusty place specializing in huts

constructed from flattened Shell oil drums. I popped my head into the first doorway that showed a tray of chipped glasses.

"*Kati?*" I inquired in Amharic and Arabic. "Do you have *kati?*"

The lady pointed at my tattered straw fedora and burst into giggles. I tried another café. The proprietor shooed me out, as did the next and the next after that. Every time I stepped out onto the street I found yet another six-foot-tall skeleton eyeing me with an ominous disinterest. Men had rifles. Women wore wildly colorful head scarfs. Ogadens, I presumed.

Suddenly, a wizened old woman, with a string of Christian crosses tattooed about her neck, beckoned me into her hut. She started babbling. She seemed frightened. I pantomimed sipping and asked about *kati*.

"*Kati?*" she asked and gestured to a sack full of dirty leaves. She repeated my drinking pantomime. "*Kati?*"

"Yes!" I pulled one of the leaves from the sack and sniffed—was this it? The legendary *kati*, *qat shia*, Abyssinian Tea, and perhaps the great-grandmother of all coffee drinks? She gestured for me to sit in a corner of the hut and then turned away. Only there was nothing in the corner to sit on. In fact, there was nothing in the hut but the bag of leaves. Was this really a café? No cups, no seats...and where was she going to cook the *kati*? How did I even know those were coffee leaves?

The old lady stopped and looked at me suspiciously.

"*Kati?*" I repeated.

"*Owwwww*," she sighed in a breathy voice.

Oh well. She looked honest enough. I crouched on the dirt floor. But what if she drugged me? There was a knock on the door, and a man in a military uniform stuck his head in. He wanted my passport. He wanted to know what the hell I was doing in Jiga-Jiga.

"Coffee," I explained lamely. "I was told to come here to

drink it."

The soldier asked the old lady a question. She shook the bag of leaves.

"You are a very stupid white man," he said angrily. "This is a restricted area—very dangerous! Please come with me."

"But...she's going to make some..." I could tell this plea was falling on deaf ears. "Of course, officer," I said coyly. "May I buy you a cup of tea first?"

"Tea?" he asked.

"No, no. I mean *kati*."

"What is that?"

I started to explain. "No. You must leave. This area is under military control."

As he loaded me onto the next van leaving for Harrar, I flashed back to the time some Irish friends were thrown out of East Harlem by two New York cops, despite their protests that they were meeting friends.

"Don't be stupid," one of the cops said after they'd escorted my friends to the nearest subway station. "You'll never have no friends here."

"THE GERMAN PRESIDENT IS COMING TO VISIT JIGA-JIGA," Abera said when I told him what had happened. "So they made you leave."

But he had good news. He'd mentioned my quest to his girlfriend. It turned out her housemate knew how to brew *kati*, and she'd invited me over for a cup.

There are actually two types of coffee-leaf beverage. The first, and more common, is *kati* or *kotea*, a concoction made of roasted coffee leaves. The other is called *amertassa*, an earlier version of the drink made from fresh-picked green leaves that are left to dry in the shade for a few days and then brewed without roasting. The market lady from whom we bought our supplies could remember her grandmother drinking *amertassa*. Now it was almost extinct. She did, however, have a burlap bag full of *kati*, broad leaves with orange and green highlights.

Kati and *amertassa* are strong candidates for being the first cup of coffee, for while Ethiopians have been eating the beans since time immemorial, the first mention of a coffee beverage suggests it was brewed from the plants' leaves. *Kafta* was its Arabic name. Some scholars claim it was brewed with leaves from the narcotic plant *qat*, yet in the early 1400s Arab mystic al-Dhabhani saw Ethiopians "using" *qahwa*, a clear reference to coffee in a liquid form. So what were the Ethiopians drinking? Quite likely a brew made from coffee leaves: the semimythical Abyssinian Tea. Raw beans were added later in southern Yemen by the Sufi mystic al-Shadhili of Mocha or one of his disciples.[2]

Whatever the case, *kati* is a lovely cuppa. Preparation is simple: dried leaves are roasted on a flat pan until they acquire a dark, tarry texture, then crumbled and brewed over low heat with water, sugar, and a pinch of salt. Cooking time is about ten minutes. The resultant amber-colored liquor has a delicately caramelized, smoky flavor comparable to lapsang souchong (Chinese smoked tea) but more complex, both sweet and salty, with a sensuously gelatinous texture.

It proved an especially sympathetic combination with the *qat* leaves Abera had bought for us to chew. *Qat* is the evil sister to coffee and has addicted much of southern Arabia and East Africa (it has also recently developed a following in the West). The two drugs' histories are so intertwined that one nickname for the

---

[2] One theory is that coffee was created as a result of Chinese Admiral Cheng Ho's supposed introduction of tea to the Arabs in the early 1400s. When China cut off contact with the outside world, the Arabs replaced tea leaves, unobtainable in Arabia, with *qat* or coffee.

patron saint of coffee drinkers, al-Shadhili of Mocha, is "the Father of Two Plants," *qat* and coffee. *Qat* is taken by chewing raw leaves and holding the pulp in the cheek until the juices are extracted. I'd first tried it years ago in Kenya and been unimpressed, but the stuff Abera brought that day was electrifying, comparable to low-key Ecstasy. Ecstasy, however, produces a physical and emotional high, whereas quality *qat*—and Harrar is said to grow the finest—gives a more cerebral euphoria, plunging the chewer into a trance-like state that makes conversation a hypnotically sensual experience.[3]

We spent the rest of the day lounging on the raised platform in Abera's traditional Harrari home. Friends came to visit. More *qat* was chewed, more *kati* was brewed, and the afternoon soon lost itself in a *qat* haze, earnest but idle, where nothing matters so much as expression and understanding. The day was hot, but Abera's clay house was cool and made comfortable with cushions. We talked about Rod Stewart, for whose haircut Abera confessed a great admiration. Later, during the more serious part of a *qat* session called Solomon's Hour, the talk turned to witchcraft. I mentioned the Ethiopian Christian deacon who had claimed Muslims used coffee to lay curses on people. Abera had never heard of this. But here in Harrar, he said, some used it for magical healing.[4]

"People come from many miles to Harrar to be healed by these people," he said.

"Have you ever seen it done?" I asked.

"Once." He shook his head. "I do not approve of these people."

"What happened? " I asked. "Did you see the Zar?"

---

[3] Tea's equivalent would be *leppet-so*, a pickled tea leaf chewed in parts of Burma.

[4] Ethiopia is a traditionally Christian nation, whereas coffee is associated with Islam, a relationship that in the past has led to the banning of coffee for Ethiopian Christians.

"You know about the Zar?"

"The priest in Addis told me. It's a devil, right?"

"No, not exactly. It is the one that comes to the *sheykah*." He asked his friend, who worked for a UN agency but spoke no English, a question. "Yes, my friend says the Zar comes to the *sheykah*. He knows all these people."

It turned out that a celebrated *sheykah* had just returned to Harrar after finishing four years of special training at Ethiopia's holy Lake Wolla, He was now holding sessions in Harrar every Tuesday and Thursday. Today was Tuesday.

"Your friend knows these holy men?" I asked.

"Yes. Some."

I hesitated. "Is it possible for a foreigner to go to a healing?"

"You wish to go?" Abera seemed surprised. "I don't know..." He asked his friend another question. "He says he does not know. No foreigners go to these things. But he can ask."

It took us the rest of the afternoon to locate the *sheykah*, only to be told that he was still asleep. It's a holiday, said his groupies; best to come back later. With presents.

"Presents?" I asked

"Yes, that is normal. It is a sign of respect."

The plan became that Abera should go alone to buy the "respect" while I went back to the hotel. We'd meet again in the evening. But in the meantime I had to give him some money to buy the presents. I wondered if it was all a scam but produced the money anyhow.

"What are you going to get them?" I asked before handing it over.

"Green coffee beans," he said. "That is what you always give. Two kilos should be enough. Don't give them anything else! You're only going to watch, not get healed."

Ethiopian Prayer

Eele buna nagay nuuklen
eele buna iijolen haagudatu
hoormati haagudatu
waan haamtu nuura dow
bokai magr nuken.

Garri/Oromo prayer

THE COFFEE BEAN HAS LONG been a symbol of power in Harrar. The caste of growers, the Harash, not only bore the city's name but were forbidden to go beyond its walls lest the art of cultivation be lost. The head of the emir's bodyguard was allowed a small private coffee garden as a sign of his rank.

And of course, natives worshiped their coffeepots, as in the prayer above, which translates

Coffeepot give us peace
coffeepot let children grow
let our wealth swell
please protect us from evils
give us rain and grass.

I think we all pray to the first cup of the day. It's a silent prayer, sung while the mind is still foggy and blue. "O Magic Cup," it might go, "carry me above the traffic jam. Keep me civil in the subway. And forgive my employer, as you forgive me. Amen."

But the prayer from the Garri/Oromo tribe is more serious, part of a ritual called *bun-qalle* that celebrates sex and death, and in which the coffee bean replaces the fatted ox in a sacrifice to the gods. Among the Garri the husking of the coffee fruit symbolizes slaughter, with the priests biting the heads off the sacrificial creatures. After this, the beans are cooked in butter and chewed by the elders. Their spiritual power thus enhanced, they pronounce a blessing on the proceedings and smear the holy coffee-scented butter on the participants' foreheads. The beans are then mixed with sweet milk, and everybody drinks the liquid while reciting the prayer.

If the whole affair seems vaguely familiar, it should. Who has gone to a business meeting where coffee is *not* offered? Its use as an intellectual lubricant, along with its ability to "swell our wealth" per the Garri prayer, has made having a pot ready for consumption an international business norm. Looked at this way, a modern business office is nothing more than a "tribe" camped out about its own sacred pot, and the *bun-qalle* is nothing less than man's first coffee klatch, archetype of the world's most common social ritual.

Two things about the *bun-qalle* mark it as probably the earliest use of coffee as a mind-altering or magical drug. The first is that the beans are fried and then eaten, a practice clearly derived from the coffee-balls chewed by Oromo warriors near Kefa. The Garri, who live a few hundred miles south of Harrar, are related to the Oromo and share their language. The second part of the ceremony, where the roasted beans are added to milk and imbibed, indicates it predates Islam (A.D. 600) because Islamic alchemists believed that mixing coffee and milk caused leprosy (a belief that lies at the root of the disdain many Europeans have for coffee with milk).

Further indication of the ceremony's extreme antiquity is the fact that the Garri associate *bun-qalle* with the sky god Waaq. His name may sound uncouth to us, but the worship of this sky god is thought to be among the world's first religions. Whether the eating of coffee beans was performed in the original Waaq ceremonies is beyond knowing. One can say, I think, that since the Garri were doubtless among the first to taste our favorite bean, and since primitive people who discover psychoactive drugs tend to worship them (a penchant today denigrated as mere substance abuse), it seems likely that consuming the beans was added to the Waaq ceremonies at a relatively early date.

In the Oromo culture of western Ethiopia, the coffee bean's resemblance to a woman's sexual organs has given birth to another *bun-qalle* ceremony with such heavy sexual significance that it is preceded by a night of abstinence, according to the work of anthropologist Lambert Bartel. Oromo elder Gammachu Magarsa told Bartel that "we compare this biting open of the coffee fruits with the first sexual intercourse on the wedding day, when the man has to force the girl to open her thighs in order to get access to her vagina."

After the beans are husked, they are stirred in the butter with a stick called *dannaba*, the word for penis. Some people replace the stick with bundles of living grass because a dead piece of wood cannot "impart life" or impregnate the beans. As the beans are stirred, another prayer is recited until finally the coffee fruits burst open from the heat, making the sound *Tass!* This bursting of the fruit is likened to both childbirth and the last cry of the dying man. The person stirring the beans now recites:

Ashama, my coffee, burst open to bring peace
there you opened your mouth
please wish me peace
keep far from me all evil tongues.

In being eaten the coffee bean "dies," blessing new thought and life, a tradition the Oromo say goes back as far as anyone can remember. After the bean has spoken, the assembly moves on to the matter at hand, such as a circumcision, marriage, land dispute, or the undertaking of a dangerous journey.

One important point about the *bun-qalle*. The beans are simply added whole to the milk, not pulverized. True infusion, where crushed beans are added to a neutral liquid like water, thus completely releasing the bean's power, is reserved for the darker acts such as laying a curse or, as in tonight's ceremony, the exorcism of an evil spirit.

"SOUNDS LIKE YOU'VE BEEN RIPPED OFF," SAID AARON.

Aaron was an American health-care expert I met while waiting for Abera to take me to the Zar ceremony.

"Forty birra," he said, referring to what I'd given Abera for the present. "Lot of money. I hope I'm wrong."

Aaron had a particularly low opinion of Ethiopians and, like any good bureaucrat, had found some studies to back up his point of view. According to these, the massive influx of international aid during the famines had made begging from foreigners the social norm. It was as natural as breathing, according to Aaron. True or not, there was no denying that urban Ethiopia was filled with a type of begging I'd only previously encountered in America—that is, people obviously in no real need striking up mock friendships merely to cadge a few birra.

"No, you'll never see your friend again," Aaron assured me. "Why don't you come up to my room and check out these baskets I bought? They were only seventy dollars each."

Abera appeared, right on time. Everything was arranged. I could attend.

"But don't give them any more presents!" he instructed again. "It is enough. And don't drink anything they give you at the ceremony."

The only disappointment was that he would not be going. He had a test to cram for. Instead his friend, a devout Catholic, had agreed to take me.

"Catholic? Will he show up?" I asked.

"He promised." Abera sounded uncertain. "Stewart, I have to ask you something. Will you be wearing your hat?"

Abera was referring to my old straw hat, the one that the first *kati* lady in Jiga-Jiga had found so amusing. You know how it is when you get so attached to a particular article of clothing that you just can't bear to throw it away? Well, I'd become very fond of this hat, a K-mart Australian style number, and over the last year of travel it had suffered considerable trauma. By the time I arrived in Ethiopia, it was little more than a crumpled piece of straw held together with half a dozen black patches. And dirty—I didn't dare wash it lest it dissolve. I loved it all the same. People in every nation reacted in a different but characteristic way. Nepalese facetiously offered large sums of money for it. Indians laughed and praised its "unique quality." The Ethiopians merely thought it unhygenic.

"You cannot wear that hat," said Abera. "Not tonight. It would be disrespectful." He pulled out an Islamic-style scarf. "Wear this. I will tie it on for you."

"Okay." I knew he was right. Besides, the scarf, white with blue and red fleur-de-lis patterns, was rather stylish. Abera tied it on, turban style.

"It looks good," he said. "You look like a Muslim."

"So I'm in disguise?"

"Maybe. Not a bad idea when you walk in Harrar late at night."

We chatted for a while. He refused my offer of dinner and, after a final exhortation to send him copies of *Cosmopolitan* Magazine (he rewrote the articles for the university paper), he departed. I sat down to wait in the hotel lobby.

Eight o'clock came and went. Then nine. Ten too. The hotel guard was spreading out his sleeping roll when there came a knock on the front door. It was Abera's friend. I thanked him for coming but asked if he thought the ceremony might be over, since we were running two hours late. No problem, he said. Nonetheless, we hurried through Harrar's darkened alleys. Squatting men called out greetings. The women, more diffident, smiled hello.

"They think you are Muslim," my friend commented, pointing to my headpiece.

As we moved out of the town's center it grew quiet. My companion fell silent. Harrar's streets are said to be haunted by spirits from all the tribes that have been enslaved here. Its hyenas, traditionally believed to be hermaphroditic, are said by some to be spirits of the poor boys castrated and sold as eunuchs. According to the eighteenth-century French traveler Antoine d'Abladie, hyenas were thought to be a type of werewolf called *buda* that attacked and ate Zar spirits.

As we approached the house where the Zar ceremony was to be held, I heard singing. The exorcism was already in progress. My companion indicated silence, and we slipped into a long, narrow room lit by a single lamp. A crowd of perhaps twenty people squatted near the door. Halfway down the room hung a dirty white sheet through which we could see the silhouette of the *sheykah* reclining on a huge brass bed. Before the sheet stood the first patient. Since we had arrived late, I was never quite clear as to the nature of this man's ailment. But the *sheykah* had already identified the possessing spirit and convinced it to leave the man in peace if he sacrificed three cocks with certain colored feathers about their necks.

A glass of pale liquor was passed around the room. People chatted in low voices. I was pleasantly surprised to be ignored. Apparently my "disguise" was working and I was being taken for some sort of foreign Muslim. Some of the people crouching by the wall began to rock slowly back and forth and sing a curious syncopated melody over and over. Incense was thrown on a brazier.

The traditional way to begin these exorcisms may include sacrificing a pair of doves or the taking of ganja or alcohol. All involve the roasting of green coffee beans, which are then chewed and brewed, thus "opening the box" and releasing the power of the *sheykah* so he can communicate with the Zar spirits, described as being toeless and having holes in their hands that, if you look through them, reveal another world. They are also said to be beautiful and come in a range of racial archetypes like Arab, white, and Chinese. The word *Zar* is thought by some to be a corruption of *Jar*, which in the Cushitic language of the Agaw tribe is the name for Waaq, the sky god.[1] Ethiopian Zar priests traditionally come from a tribe called Wato or Wallo, the name of the lake where tonight's priest was trained and Ethiopia's most ancient holy spot. The Wallo tribe claims to be the descendants of the original Oromo coffee chewers and at

[1] In the Rastafarian religion, which derives from Ethiopia, God is referred to as Jah.

one point were so feared for their magical powers that other tribes dared not molest them. Until recently it was customary to plant a coffee tree on the graves of particularly powerful sorcerers, and the Oromo say that the first coffee tree grew from the tears of the sky god as they fell on the body of a dead wizard.

I've called this ceremony an exorcism, but it's really a negotiation between the Zar and the *sheykah*, who alone can communicate with the Zar and, if necessary, bargain them down to more reasonable requests. The role of coffee is perhaps comparable to the peyote "allies" popularized in Carlos Castaneda's *Way of Knowledge* trilogy, inasmuch as the "spirits" within the bean can only function according to the abilities of the person who has taken them into his or her body.

A girl came forward and placed more gifts on the ground before the *sheykah*'s silhouette. She suffered from headaches, it seemed, terrible, horrible headaches that would last for days. As she talked, the *sheykah*'s silhouette could be seen shivering.

The girl stopped and stood mute while her narration of woes was picked up by a male relative. From his description, it appeared her difficulties were more serious than headaches.

"It is a problem in the head," whispered Abera's friend.

She'd been having fits and strange, violent seizures in which she destroyed furniture. The family had decided to consult the Zar priest when she had tried to bite off her mother's finger. The audience moaned as her tale unfolded. Her symptoms indicated classic evil Zar possession. The Zar tend to inhabit women, whom they mount like a horse and force to perform unnatural acts, including self-mutilation with iron bars, the scars of which invariably disappear by morning.

Suddenly the girl threw herself to the ground and started yelling, clutching her head, and shivering as if in great pain. It grew more and more pronounced as the *sheykah* questioned the evil spirit within her. During all this, my Catholic friend shook his head in disgust. Finally it was decided the girl's family would donate a calf. Then the girl's Zar made a highly unusual demand: she must cut off all her hair and go alone to scatter the strands in the fields where the hyenas waited.

A pair of scissors was fetched. But when they began to cut, the girl pointed to where we sat. Apparently my disguise was not as good as I'd thought. She did not want a foreigner to witness her shearing.

As we trudged back to the hotel, Abera's friend explained things I had not understood. He had a low regard for the proceedings. I mentioned that in America we had similar healers on TV.

"They too use coffee beans?" he asked.

"Well, coffee is certainly popular among them," I explained. "But for payment they generally prefer credit cards."

I was told the next day that all traces of the girl's hair had vanished from the fields by sunrise.

ONCE THE ETHIOPIANS DISCOVERED COFFEE'S PSYCHEDELIC powers, it was only a question of time before their neighbors caught on. By some accounts it was the pharaonic Egyptians to the north who first got hooked, with some overexcited scholars speculating that Egypt's legendary nepenthe, consumed by Helen of Troy to "ease her sorrows," was an early form of the Frappuccino.

But the main direction the coffee bean headed from Harrar was east to the Red Sea, then by boat to the port of al-Makkha, also known as Mocha, in what is today the nation of Yemen. There was a fair amount of trading going on between Harrar and al-Makkha back in the first millennium. Mainly ostrich feathers, rhinoceros horn, and tortoiseshell. The essentials. And slaves, of course. The Arabs were notorious slave traders and roamed this area in search of the victims they called *zanj*. The *zanj* were fond of the Arabs, or at least of their sweets. "The *zanj* held the [Arabs] in awe, prostrating themselves and calling out, 'Greetings, O People from the Land of Dates!' " according to the medieval Arab writer Kitab al-Agail al-Hind. "For those who travel to this country steal the children of the *zanj* with sweet dates, luring them from place to place [with sight of the sweets] and then taking possession of them and carrying them off to their own countries."

A thousand years ago it took the slave caravans up to twenty days to travel from Harrar to the Red Sea coast. Boys destined for the Turkish harems were castrated on the roadside. At least half of the captives died. The coffee trees sprouted from their leftovers.

My own journey to the Red Sea took only three days. I hitched from Harrar to the town of Dire Dawa near the country's sole railroad. The train was a day late in arriving, but worth the wait; a baby blue, turn-of-the-century French *chemin de fer* with old-fashioned reclining seats (at least in first class) whose upholstery had disintegrated into filthy shreds. Mechanical failures turned the twelve-hour journey into a two day ordeal. As I had just spent a year in India, these kinds of delays seemed perfectly natural; I merely closed my eyes and pretended to be dead (or maybe I was just wishing).

We finally disembarked in the port of Djibouti, a town the thirteenth-century Islamic pilgrim Ibn Battuta described as "the dirtiest, most disagreeable and most stinking town in the world," whose citizens had a taste for camel flesh. Today Djibouti is technically a nation. In reality, it's a glorified French military post bursting with bars and brothels. My first stop was a café for a cold drink.

"You speak English?" A big-bellied man in a plaid skirt, a *kanga*, had seated himself at the next table. "*Tu parles français?*"

"Yes."

He studied my hat. "Ah—an American man. Good! I speak *twelve* languages," he informed me. "I have sailed to every port in all the world—Cairo, Alexandria, Venice, New York, Athens, Sydney, Hong Kong..."

The list continued. He was a retired sailor.

"And so I have returned to 'Jibouti. You like?" I raised my eyebrows in a grimace of pleasure. "Why have you come?" he asked.

I explained I was looking for a boat going to al-Makkha.

He looked at me in surprise. "Al-Makkha? Why do you go there?"

"Coffee."

"You go to Yemen for coffee?" he translated for the crowd at the bar. Everybody burst into laughter. "Not many boats are going there today, my friend."

He explained that just yesterday Eritrea had invaded a group of Yemeni islands located midway between the two countries. The Red Sea was crawling with armies from both sides, and the Yemen air force had reportedly been bombing suspicious-looking vessels.

"But you are lucky. My friend's boat leaves today. Some people, they have waited two weeks and will not worry about the bombs. But you must hurry!"

His friend's boat turned out to be a thirty-foot long vessel whose brightly painted hull had long ago faded to gray. There was a hut, of sorts, toward the rear, and a rudimentary mast (no sail), but not much else. There was no radio, no light, and no emergency equipment of any kind. The toilet was a box hanging over the ocean. There wasn't even a deck, just a jumble of crates covered with a green tarp, across which were scattered fifteen Somali refugees.

But it floated. Captain Abdou Hager and I quickly settled on thirty dollars. I hopped aboard, and five minutes later the *Qasid*

Karin shook the rats off its lines and set off. It was that hour in the evening when the sun sinks out of sight, sending thick, buttery golden rays across the sky. The sea turned dark purple. Tomorrow, I thought, I'll be in Yemen. As we reached the harbor mouth, the ship slowed. There was a splash, and the engine went off.

"There is too much wind," explained a fourteen-year-old Somali boy next to me. "We go tomorrow."

His name was Mohammed. He and his sister were being sent to live with relatives in Yemen until the war ended. He was beautiful, I suppose, slender and tall with incredibly large feminine eyes and pouting lips. If he'd been dressed in a woman's clothes, I would have taken him for a young girl. He asked if America had warlords like the ones in Somalia. Oh yes, I said, all the big cities had warlords. He and his sister, Ali, seemed surprised. Did the American warlords have tanks and guns? they wanted to know. Not so many tanks, I said, but lots of guns. I assured them that many neighborhoods in America were indistinguishable from Mogadishu.

After a few minutes of chatting, Mohammed, who spoke very limited English (though better than my Somali), gave me a present.

"I want you to have this," he said, placing a wad of Somali money in my hands. "Take."

I objected. Somali refugees shouldn't give cash to American tourists. Quite the opposite. And I had absolutely no intention of handing out handfuls of American money in return.

"No, no, no," I said. "You shouldn't do that."

"Yes, yes." He thrust the money back into my hands. "Take."

"It's very pretty," I said. It came to about fifteen thousand Somali shillings. "I cannot take this. You're a crazy man."

An Ethiopian who spoke better English intervened. The

Somali government no longer existed. The money was worthless. I reluctantly accepted the pretty pieces of paper. Mohammed appeared mystified as to why I would only accept his gift if I thought it was worthless.

Ali was also distraught, mainly because in Yemen she would be obliged to don the veil. She pulled the hem of her robe over her face mockingly.

"Bad, bad," she said. "Not in my country."

Her face was a wonderful mix of Arab and African features. She plied me with tea and biscuits. I gave her my Arab-English dictionary.

Around two in the morning they pulled out their prized possession, a Casio minikeyboard. I played them the opening to Mozart's Sonata in A, but they were more interested in the machine's auto-rhythm controls, which produced a steady syncopation in whatever style you selected. In the days when coffee made this journey, these two would have been bound for slavery, I thought, listening to the tinselly bossa novas thumping against the wind. Now they were only refugees; I wondered if that qualified as a real improvement.

Sailing to al-Makkha

In his travels he passed by a coffee bush and nourished himself, as is the custom of the pious, on its fruit which he found untouched. He found that it made his brain nimble, promoting wakefulness for the performance of religious duties.

al-Kawakib al-sa'irn bi-a'yan al-mi'a al-'ashira
by Najm al-Din al-Ghazzi (1570–1651)

THE SHIP'S MOTOR WOKE ME in the morning. Djibouti had disappeared, and, peering over the railing, all I could see was a heaving sea of turquoise water flecked with whitecaps. It was like looking into a shattered mirror reflecting the sky. It didn't seem to me that the windstorm had died down at all.

I noticed that the others had moved their belongings to the lean-to at the rear of the boat. I decided to stay where I was. A wave crashed over the bow and drenched me from head to foot. Another wave crashed over, and another. I was still moving my belongings to the rear with the others', when I noticed that the deck had started to tilt at a twenty-degree angle.

The *Qasid* stopped moving forward. The crew had turned the ship's nose out of the wind while they bailed water out of the hold and got the ship righted. Boxes were shifted about, and I decided the problem was only that the cargo's weight had been poorly distributed. Then a fishing vessel came racing by, and I noticed how high it was riding. The *Qasid* was riding about seven feet lower. Our captain had overloaded the boat.

We set out and immediately waves started crashing over the bow. Again, we pulled over and bailed. This continued all day. Finally our crew became concerned that the cargo of "cookies" might be damaged by the salt water. The real problem, however, was that the *Qasid* was carrying mainly booze and AK-47s.

The booze was from Djibouti, but the guns, I was later told, were returning to Yemen after an unsuccessful sales trip to Eritrea. The weight of all those weapons was pulling us down.

The crew decided to find an island and wait out the gale. I write "the crew" because I realize now that I never saw Captain Abdou on board. No matter. The three teenagers and two old men who manned the *Qasid* soon had us anchored next to an island. All of us immediately hung our belongings out to dry. I noted that even here, out of the wind, the gale kept the clothes flapping at a ninety-degree angle. It was, I suppose, really the Red Sea equivalent of an interstate rest stop. But, technically, we were now shipwrecked on a desert island. I was rather pleased. After all the boat's engine still ran. We'd probably get to Yemen eventually.

Some of my fellow passengers, however, were less sanguine about the situation. Paulious, for instance, an Ethiopian *qat* addict. Habitual chewers deprived of their daily mouthful are haunted by the demon *katou*, and Paulious was perturbed at being stranded in such an obviously *qat*-free environment.

"Oh, bad thoughts will come," he kept whining. "We have to leave."

The first fight broke out between an ancient sailor, whom I'd dubbed "the Toothless One," and a passenger who had tried to steal his *qat*. The others quickly pulled them apart—Toothless had been threatening the young man with his flip-flop—but it was a bad omen. Toothless had earned his sobriquet when I'd noticed him grinding up a green purée in some sort of mill. At first I'd thought he was preparing food. Later I realized that it was his precious *qat*. Being toothless, he had to first "chew" it with this mechanical device in order to extract the leaf's precious juices.

There was another crew member, a boy of perhaps sixteen, with curly hair, whom I'd caught staring at me a number of times. He had an honest, open face that bordered on simple, and a monkey-like way of moving that made me think he must have spent his life on boats like the *Qasid*. I was talking with the others and the word *America* came up. The boy, who was sitting on the crate above us, pointed in puzzlement toward al-Makkha.

"He is from al-Merica?" he inquired of the others. "Is that near al-Makkha?"

The others laughed, Paulious loudest of all. "He doesn't even know what America is!" he said.

"Is it an island?" the boy asked.

I pointed northwest. "It's over there."

"By Eritrea?"

The others laughed again.

"No, no. It's very far," I said. "If you were to go there, you would come first to Eritrea, then Ethiopia, than all of Africa and Turkey and then Europe and then there's another place, England, and the sea beyond that. A great sea. Beyond all that," I said, "that's where America is." The others translated.

The boy looked at me as if he just couldn't understand how a place could be that far away.

"It's not as far as it sounds," I said lamely.

He looked even more confused. Then his eyes narrowed—the others were still laughing. I think he thought that they were laughing at him and that I was lying, making fun of him. He moved away, with a look wavering between anger and puzzlement, and suddenly I thought, yes, he was right, it was impossibly far. Too far to go, and even if such a voyage was possible, why would anybody want to go so far from home? And why should he care about a place that might as well be on the moon? He, the boy, lived here. He had lived here all his life, probably on this very boat; this was his home, this and al-Makkha and the sand and the sea and the wind and the waiting. And one day he would be the Toothless One sitting by the mast, laughing and stealing orange cream cookies from the cargo. He would be thirty, maybe forty, but he would look much, much older.

After that, whenever I smiled at him he moved away. He referred to me only as the American, as did all the others. I spent the rest of the afternoon sitting alone.

The port we were headed for, al-Makkha in Yemen, is still one of the world's most isolated areas. But back when coffee was brought there by kidnapped Africans, it verged on mythical, at least to Westerners. "Terrifically unhealthy even to sail by" was how the first-century Greek author of the *Periplus Maris Erypraei* described it. "A land full of ichthyophagoi [fish eaters] who plunder and enslave any who are shipwrecked there." The Greeks believed that Arabs ate huge lizards and boiled their fat down for oil. Winged dragons were said to guard the coast, which was believed to be contaminated by horrific diseases.

Much of this propaganda was spread by the Arabs to

discourage raiders from attacking the myrrh fields that were crucial to their trading empire. Using ships similar to the *Qasid*, Arab sailors from Oman were already bringing indigo, diamonds, and sapphires from India. To Africa they carried "weapons from Muza [al-Makkha] of local craftsmanship to gain the good will of the savages." Back from Africa, they transported civet, musk, tortoiseshell, and rhino horn.

And slaves, lots of them, some of whom introduced coffee seeds to Arabia. Numbers are woefully inexact, but *zanj* slaves were in China by the first century. In 1474, eight thousand African slaves briefly took over Bengal in eastern India. This slave trade reached its apex when Oman's Black Sultanate ousted the Portuguese and set up headquarters in Zanzibar, circa 1800, enslaving almost half of the population on the Swahili (eastern) coast of Africa.

We had rice for dinner. There seemed to be flickering lights coming from the direction of the Hanish Islands. I asked if it might be planes dropping bombs. The others said no, it was nothing. Everyone fell into a sullen silence except Paulious, who was getting positively twitchy over the lack of *qat*. He kept babbling to me how it was good, that the wind was dying, we could go soon. I pointed out the mini sand storms dancing in the darkness atop the island's ridge, causing trails of silvery starlight to run down the face of the sky.

"Is *al-sichan*," he said, giving the dust devils their Ethiopian name. "Bad things will happen."

The next day the wind had calmed enough for us to go on. We spied land around sunset and several hours later we dropped anchor just outside the port of al-Makkha. When we tried to dock the next morning, however, we found that Yemen didn't want us. My fellow passengers, mainly Somali refugees, had no official papers. We were told to anchor twenty-five yards from the dock and stay put, forbidden to arrive, forbidden to leave.

For three days and nights we drifted among the port's derelict ships. Friendships formed and fell apart. More fights broke out. The Somali boy, Mohammed, refused to speak. When I asked what was the matter, he would only look up at the stars and murmur, "Ees so beautiful."

HE WAS RIGHT. DURING THE DAY WE COULD SEE THE BONE-WHITE minarets of al-Makkha appearing and disappearing among swirling sandstorms. At night, I lay on my back and watched the stars spin round and round overhead as our boat swung about its anchoring point. Nights were cold. I had no blanket, so I sang Billie Holiday songs to stay warm. When I carried the tune, the Toothless One would reward me with a pack of biscuits. His favorite was "God Bless the Child."

My psyche began vomiting up every memory it could get its claws on. Phantom Christmas carols flitted on the winds, and I repeated certain sexual fantasies so often I could feel my lover's hair curled about my fingers. On the last night I became aware of activity on a nearby wreck. It was half submerged, and I'd assumed it was abandoned. But that night I kept seeing pastel lights flickering from its portholes. Every time our boat swung close by, I would rise on one elbow and peer through the darkness. Someone in the wreck was watching Michael Jackson videos, the "Billy Jean" one with the glowing footsteps. It was hard to be sure, what with the constant motion and my salt-crusted glasses, but I was convinced that Michael Jackson was doing his moonwalk across the water, over and over and over...

On the third day I woke to find the *Qasid* pulling up to the dock. The Somali women went behind the veil. My shipmates were loaded into a pickup truck, but I was taken to a small shack surrounded by soldiers wearing checkered Arabian head scarves. Inside was another soldier seated behind a desk.

"Passport."

I handed it over. He flipped through the pages angrily.

"So," he said without looking up. "You have just come from…"

"Ethiopia."

"Djibouti, it says. Which is it?"

"Yes, yes, Djibouti," I said. "I forgot."

He snorted. "You forgot Djibouti. Have you also forgotten the war?"

"The war? Between Yemen and Eritrea? Of course not."

"Of course not." He leaned back in his chair. "Strange that you, an American, should be here now. Do you know why I say this?"

It seemed that the war was not going well. The Eritreans had driven the Yemenese off the Hanish Islands. Fifty or so people had died. Serious. And, according to the officer, the whole thing had started when the Eritreans signed over seabed drilling rights to an American oil company. The seabed had been between Eritrea's shoreline and the islands, so Eritrea had invaded to strengthen its oil claim.

And now here I was, an American in a funny hat. I was obviously from the CIA.

"So you have come to al-Makkha," he said, bobbing his head and smiling at me.

"Did you find my visa?" I asked.

"Ah yes," he said scornfully. "The visa." He pointed to my belongings, spread out on a table by the wall. "You have camera?"

"Yes."

"You take pictures?"

"Not in al-Makkha." I tried to sound outraged. "This is a military zone!"

"Ah. But why have you come to al-Makkha?"

"Coffee," I explained.

"Coffee? In al-Makkha?"

"Yes. You know, al-Shadhili..."

"The mosque?" He reopened my passport and examined the first page. "But it does not say here you are a Muslim."

"No, but..."

"Only Muslims may enter the mosque."

"I only want to see...just look..."

"Oh. First you say you come for coffee. Now you say you are a tourist." He did not believe me. "Yet you come to Yemen with criminals from Eritrea. With a camera."

So he was going to lock me up as a spy. Fine with me, I thought. As long as there's a bed and running water. It might be interesting watching Yemenese bureaucracy run its course. He would send a description, they would have more questions, he would send answers. More questions, more answers, but we both knew that eventually I would be freed.

The official studied me. Perhaps he saw the images in my mind because suddenly he seemed to decide I wasn't worth the effort. He made a gesture I came to identify with Yemenese philosophy: he raised his right hand to his ear and made a curious flinging-away gesture with his thumb and first two fingers while rolling his eyes heavenward. Then he ordered two machine-gun-toting soldiers to escort me out.

"Welcome. Don't forget your passport." He handed it over. "But if you have come for coffee you are three hundred years too late."

THE PORT OF AL-MAKKHA HAS BEEN SYNONYMOUS WITH COFFEE for almost a thousand years. It was here that the first beans arrived from Africa, and *al-Makkha*, corrupted to *Mocha*, later became the universal nickname for the brew. It was also in Mocha, around 1200, that an Islamic hermit named al-Shadhili apparently brewed the first mug. Although Ethiopians were already chewing the bean, and perhaps making a tea from its leaves, al-Shadhili of Mocha is thought by most to be the first to have made a coffee bean drink.

"It has reached us from many people," said Fakhr al-Din al-Makki, "that the first one to introduce *qahwa* [coffee] and to make its use a widespread and popular [custom] in the Yemen was our master Shaykh... 'ali ibn 'Umar al-Shadhili, one of the masters of the Shadhilya order."

There are as many stories about how al-Shadhili made his discovery as there are ways to spell his name. He discovered coffee while walking home from prayers one night; no, he was actually fasting in the wilderness when he discovered the plant's powers. Some say he lived on nothing but coffee beans for twenty years; others go so far as to claim it was the Archangel Gabriel who revealed that a java-only diet would lead to sainthood. In the oddest version, our hero is unjustly accused of playing footsie with the king's daughter and banished to the wilderness, where he lives on coffee beans until the Archangel Gabriel reveals to him that the ruler has been struck down by a skin disease that al-Shadhili can cure with a cup of the magic brew.

Some historical accounts have him, or one of his brethren, visiting Ethiopia, where he observes people drinking coffee and then brings back the habit. Later accounts toss in how a shipload of seasick Portuguese sailors pulled into Mocha. Ill and malnourished, they were on the point of death until the kindly al-Shadhili advised them to try the magic potion he had been drinking for years. The sailors tried it and within days were well enough to set sail. As they departed, al-Shadhili is said to have cried out to them, "Remember this, the drink of al-Makkha!" And so the drink that changed history was introduced to the West, and Mocha's fame was forever assured.

Whatever. In fact, the Shadhilis are a Sufi sect, and from 1200 to 1500 a handful of Shadhili dervishes wandered around the Arabian peninsula having coffee-scented religious experiences. The group eventually spread as far as Spain, where a syncretic Christian/Muslim group called al-Shadhiliya yet exists, and is so closely associated with coffee that you still ask for a cup of al-Shadhili in Algeria. All anyone really knows is that a member of the Shadhiliya order introduced coffee to the world, that one of them lived in al-Makkha (Mocha), and that whatever it was they drank, it was probably dreadful since they didn't roast their beans. It seems they may have made a stew of raw beans, leaves, and cardamom. Indeed, there is some evidence that all al-Shadhili of Mocha really did was make a tea from *qat* leaves, and that it was another Sufi in Aden who later replaced the leaves with beans.

From this humble start grew a small empire. By the 1400s, when the Turks conquered Yemen, coffee from Mocha was being drunk throughout the Islamic world. When the first English trader visited the port, in 1606, almost half a century before Europe's first café opened, he reported that there were over thirty-five merchant ships from as far away as India crowding the harbor, all waiting for the bags of coffee that cluttered the docks. In a pleasant reversal from the present currency exchange, the English merchant John Jourdain wrote that Mocha was full of "all kinds of commodities that are so deare that there is no dealing for us...at the rates they sell them to the merchants from Great Cairo." Coffee palaces lined the harbor, and princes sat on gold cushions, fanned by hordes of slaves. There was even a private army whose job was to ensure that no infidel stole one of the precious coffee plants.

By then, the long-dead hermit al-Shadhili had been dubbed the patron saint of coffee drinkers, and his tomb, located in a local mosque, had become a destination for Islamic pilgrims.

I'd seen the minaret while we were being held in the harbor, and as soon as the authorities let me go, I headed for it. Modern Mocha turned out to be the grubbiest, most fly-infested hellhole I had ever seen. Men in rags, their feet black with oil, lounged about on the vulture-picked motorcycle carcasses that made up the local taxi fleet. There were a few fishy smelling cafés and a *funduq* hotel with thirty men crammed into a single room. The monsoon wind that had harried our ship was still blowing, only here it kicked up a small sandstorm. Within a minute I was covered in rivulets of sand and sweat that slowly dripped down the inside of my shirt.

When I finally reached the old part of the town, a quote from a book I'd seen in India came to mind.

"The city presented itself as a very beautiful object," Jean de La Roque wrote in his *Voyage to Arabia the Happy*. "There were many palm trees and palaces... The sight much rejoiced us."

It had been written three hundred years ago. I realized things might have changed. But this, I thought, standing at the end of the town's single road, this was unbelievable. As far as the horizon stretched a sandy plain dotted with ruined mansions. Immediately to my left stood the shattered walls of a coffee merchant's palace straight out of *The Arabian Nights*, replete with elaborately carved friezes and balconies and onion-shaped windows. Further afield stood a crenellated tower that must once have been the corner of a small fortress. The ruins—some little more than a shattered wall—appeared to stretch for miles. In between them were dozens of small hills of sand that, I later realized, hid the remains of even more buildings.

The only sign of life was an ancient man squatting next to a crumbling wall, apparently unaware of my presence.

"*Salaam*," I called out. He continued sucking on his hookah. Perhaps he's deaf, I thought, and went to stand in his line of vision. Nothing. Now, I've seen some grisly characters before, but this guy took the cake. His clothes hung in oil-stained rags that looked like they'd come straight from the mechanic's shop, and his turban was so caked with grease and dirt it must have held its shape in perpetuity. His skin looked mummified, a violent, sunburnt brown splintered into a spiderweb of wrinkles. The sweat pouring down from under his turban left tracks in the sand clinging to his face. His hookah matched him to a tee, being an ingenious contraption of rusted pipes stuck in a broken water bottle, with a sardine can standing in for the pipe's bowl.

I pointed to the mosque inquiringly. "Al-Shadhili?"

I could hear his pipe gurgle as he took another hit. Still no reaction. I wandered over to the mosque to see if I could find a way in. It was a cluster of six low-lying domes from the midst of which leapt a forty-foot-tall white minaret covered in the elegant geometrical carvings of the Zabid school. (Zabid is a nearby village where algebra was born.) I went around to the other side and found a wooden door covered with brass knobs. Before I could knock, however, an old fellow popped out. He gave me a grin, whirled on his heel, slapped a padlock in place, and disappeared into the sandstorm before I could so much as hiss, "Baksheesh!"

I studied the mosque for a second. Then the ruins. The old man smoking the hookah. Through the wind I caught a whiff of something rank. It was me. I hadn't taken a shower in a week. I was starving and weak, and my head was pounding from what felt like a shattered tooth. The sandstorm was so bad I had to keep my hand over my glass lenses to keep them from being destroyed. I decided to leave.

"Bye now," I said. "See ya later."

The old man took another puff from his hookah and stared straight ahead. I set off into the sandstorm to find a way out of al-Makkha.

An Evil Sister

The imams complained their mosques were empty while the coffee houses were always full.

Alexandre Dumas

It was fifteen minutes to midnight as my ride pulled into Yemen's highland capital of Sana'a. I'd made it, I thought. A scrap of paper blew across the deserted square. Whoopee.

My car came to a halt.

"Sleep?" said the driver's teenage boy. He pointed to the only lit doorway on the street.

"Hotel?" I inquired.

The boy nodded. His father, wearing a checkered Arab

headpiece, leaned back to confirm once more that Yemen was indeed Number One. Absolutely, I said, handing him the fare. He gave me the thumbs-up and roared off into the dark

I started climbing the hotel's stairwell. Was Yemen really Number One? I was not as certain as I'd led my driver to believe. Actually, I knew almost nothing about the place, since the only guidebook I'd been able to locate in Ethiopia was nine years out of date. It boasted that Yemen was the most isolated of the Islamic nations, its citizens were all drug addicts, and its highland capital, Sana'a, where I now stood, had really weird buildings. I turned a bend in the stairwell and found a boy in a gray body-length robe watching me from the second floor. In one hand he held a flickering candle. In the other, he held a sprig of leaves. As we discussed room price, he nibbled the tenderest buds. *Qat*. The boy noted my glance and offered me a leaf. I declined. He led me down a hallway to my quarters. It was a pleasant room but, like everything else, unpolluted by electrical current. I flicked the light switch to be sure.

"Lights?" I inquired, pointing to the ceiling fixture.

The boy spread his hands and looked heavenward.

"*Bismillah*," he said.

Allah willing, I translated in my head. Right. I shooed him off and sat down to consider the day. It had started well enough. After leaving al-Shadhili's tomb, I'd gone to al-Makkha's main road and found a station-wagon taxi waiting. There were already eleven men crammed inside, which meant there was room for one more.

"We go!" shouted the driver in English as I settled into the rear compartment. "Bring those goats here. We put them in the back with the American."

My eyes widened—six goats! The driver laughed and slammed the door shut.

"Ha-ha!" he shouted. "This is joke!"

Unfortunately his estimate of a six-hour journey proved to be yet another bit of wit. The trip took over twelve, albeit well spent as the ride turned into a live demonstration of the single most important social force in Yemen, the drug *qat*.

"It's the worst thing that's happened to Yemen," said a fellow passenger by the name of Galal. "Worse even than the British."

"Worse than the British?" I said. "Hard to imagine."

I was already familiar with *qat* from Ethiopia. But according to Galal, who'd lived in Europe and Mecca, the drug had addicted so many Yemen men that it was destroying the economy and threatening to eliminate coffee from the land that had first cultivated it.

"It started first in the afternoon. People would chew *qat* for an hour after lunch and then go back to work. Then it grew to three hours. After a whole afternoon of chewing, you don't really want to go back to the office, especially if you are in the government. Now, many people, they come to work worn out from chewing the day before, and all they do is think about getting more *qat*, and then, about ten in the morning, they rush off to the *qat* market to make sure they get the best. Then they go chew, and soon the day is over and nothing is done."

We were driving through a stunning landscape of biblical mountains and cliffhanging villages and castles. It was here, near Taiz and Ibb in southern Yemen, that coffee was first cultivated eight hundred years ago on the legendary Nasmurade (Nakil Sumara), or Coffee Mountain. The Yemenese had convinced Europeans that coffee would grow only on Nasmurade, according to English traveler John Jourdain, writing in 1616, because "it was the highest mountain in Arabie...[on top of which stood] two fortresses guarding their most precious commodity that is carried to Great Cairo."

Not anymore. The rippling mountainside terraces, some of which date back before Christ, now grow nothing but *qat*. This progression is indicative of the historic relationship between the two drugs. In fact, the cup brewed by the Sufi al-Shadhili of Mocha is thought by some to have been a tea made of *qat* leaves, which another Sufi named al-Dhabhani replaced with coffee beans because *qat* was unavailable in his town of Aden. Both are stimulants, but *qat*, often called coffee's evil sister, is also a narcotic, and so unusual a substance that it is the sole occupant of one of the World Health Organization's seven categories for drugs. The American government considers it as dangerous a substance as heroin.

The area near Ibb is said to produce the finest *qat* in Yemen, second only to Harrar's, and boys hawking bunches of bright green leaves dotted the highway. Our driver stopped at every one. Galal pointed out all the varieties, such as *sawli*, or truck driver's *qat*, which sometimes produces horrible crawling sensations, and *shami*, the *qat* of poets, bunches of tender buds packed in banana leaves. *Qat* grown on graves is said to produce hallucinations.

Galal, who worked as a bank manager in Dubai, also pointed out that our driver took in about twelve hundred riyadhs in fares for the day but spent at least eight hundred on *qat*. Many men spend three quarters of their income on the drug, he said. I'd noticed that every village market had a *qat* section as large as all the others combined.

"Ah, but for real prestige some grow their own tree," said Galal. "Only then can one be sure it is of the freshest!"

By evening everyone in our taxi was high on *qat* except me and a Koran-toting Sudanese—including Galal, who'd been castigating *qat* through lips stained green by the drug. Why chew, I asked, if he held it in such low esteem?

He explained he was considering moving back to Yemen. "I don't want people to think I'm strange."

But that was over, I thought, climbing into my hotel's surprisingly comfortable bed. I snuffed out the candle. So what if Yemen was full of *qat*-heads? Surely here in the capital, Sana'a, the bean would predominate. I closed my eyes and repeated the only Arabic phrase I knew—*qahwa al-bon*. *Bon* is Arabic for bean; *qahwa*, wine. "The Wine of the Bean."

MORNING CAME, AND I HIT THE MARKET OF OLD SANA'A, THE *SUQ* (pronounced "sook"), Arabic for shopping mall. Sana'a has the world's oldest, a maze of medieval alleyways bursting with crystallized dates ("Greetings, O People from the Land of Dates!") and raisins and myrrh and incense, spare wheels, guns, moneychangers, Korean girlie dresses, cologne, shoelaces, aftershave lotion, Islamic prayer beads, hookahs, and teapots made from old tin cans. *Suq* till you puke, as the locals say. And there was coffee too, brown-and-white striped burlap bags brimming with the bean.

"*Qahwa?*" I asked.

The shop owner looked up at me skeptically.

"*Qahwa?*" I repeated the Arabic word. "*Qahwa al-bon?*" He gestured to the bags. "No, no." I made drinking motions. "To drink."

"Drink? You want to drink coffee?" he said in English, then gestured to a crowd of men drinking on the other side of the alley. Like everybody else, they were wearing checkered headpieces and ankle-length shirts. A foot-long curved dagger was tucked into each man's belt. Of course, said the coffee-stall proprietor when I tottered over. We have coffee. But not now. Later. Tomorrow. Would I like some tea? One man pointed me toward San Sarat al'Muzan, the coffee *suq*. Perhaps there, he said with a friendly shove into the crowd. I immediately lost my way.

It was the same at every stall I tried. Coffee? Now? Impossible. They all told me to return tomorrow. How could it be so difficult to get a cup of coffee in the markets of Yemen? Was I pronouncing the word incorrectly? Kahwah, koowah, keeqay, keeah...I started muttering variations to myself as I wandered from stall to stall. How many ways could you pronounce the wretched thing?

Sana'a is like a sand castle built by a kid on LSD, a car-free maze of seven-story mud skyscrapers covered in whimsical white plaster friezes. There's nothing like it, and for a while I lost myself in the pleasure of mindless gawking. Then I smelled The Smell, wafting through the market's thousand other scents, the unmistakable aroma of roasting coffee. Drawn irresistibly, I plunged through a huge arch and into a courtyard full of merchants lounging over hundreds of bags filled with a small dark fruit. Raisins. I rushed back to the main alley and followed the aroma to yet another *suq*, this one dotted with yard-high pyramids of ginger, cloves, cardamom, and cinnamon. I groaned. The spice market. Now I'd never find the scent again.

"*Qahwa?*" I inquired of one of the merchants, and a moment later I was in an ancient cobblestone courtyard walled on three sides with stacks of fifty-kilo coffee bags. A man with a waist-length beard sat cross-legged, correcting an enormous ledger. A boy watched me from a doorway. Then I heard a faint rhythmic scrutching coming from a doorway in the courtyard's corner. Inside sat two men up to their shoulders in piles of unhusked coffee beans. They were tossing the toasted beans into large metal-mesh baskets to separate the husks. The only modern devices in sight were a dilapidated coffee roaster and a single bare lightbulb.

San Salat al' Musan. The world's oldest coffee *suq*. I removed my shoes and sat on the doorstep to stare at the two men. They were all smiles. I indicated I wanted to touch some beans and then plunged my hand into a pile of the darkly gleaming bodies. This is better than drinking it, I thought as they slid over my skin in a sensuous cascade. I plunged my other arm in up to the elbow. Much better, I thought; no need for a cup.

The boy appeared bearing a trio of tumblers brimming with a dark, steaming liquid. The men tossed aside their baskets with cries of delight and grabbed two of the cups. The boy proffered the third to me. Ah, I thought, raising the glass to my lips—at last! In the Holy of Holies, surrounded by mountains of the Blessed Bean, taking a cup of that brew most beloved by the Prophet, the thrice-blessed wine of Islam.

"*Shia?*" asked the boy, pointing to my glass. "*Shia*—you like some tea?"

SHE CAME TO PROVE SOLOMON WITH HARD QUESTIONS AT Jerusalem, with a very great company and camels that bore spices...neither were there any such spices as the Queen of Sheba gave King Solomon.

It's a shame that the above passage from the Bible neglects to mention which spices the queen bestowed upon Solomon. Certainly there would have been frankincense and myrrh, since Sheba, or Saba, was one of Yemen's earliest kingdoms, and those were its most famous exports. Were coffee beans among these precious gifts? Perhaps, according to historians who believe that the kingdom of Sheba included Ethiopia. The only evidence offered is that Solomon forced himself on the queen that night, thus giving birth to the rumor that the bean was an aphrodisiac. It is also worth noting that Arabic historian Abu al-Tayyib al-Ghazzi (1570–1651), writing at a time when coffee was only beginning to gain widespread popularity outside Yemen, also associated Solomon with *qahwa*, by claiming that soon after the queen's visit he used coffee beans from "the Yemen" to cure a plague-ridden town.

The generally accepted theory is that coffee came into use among the Arabs a few centuries after the birth of Islam. Most Westerners today associate Islam with terrorists, bearded fanatics, and a distressing lack of toilet paper. This, of course, is both silly and true. Islam is a beautiful religion. Of course it's not perfect—any religion that insists half the species walk about with a bag over their head clearly has some issues to deal with—but in its heyday it was the crowning glory of the human race. While the Christians in Europe were sunk in the Dark Ages, Muslims were studying Aristotle, inventing algebra, and generally creating one of the most elegant civilizations in history.

But who cares? The main thing is they were all teetotalers. Denied the pleasures of the grape, it's hardly surprising that this new society took to coffee with a passion, particularly the mystic Sufis, who began using it in their religious ceremonies.

"Bullshit. Awesome bullshit. Sufis!" Ishmael, my tablemate at a local café, was a Sunni Muslim and apparently had little time for Sufism, or, for that matter, Islam in general. "The only thing the people in this country do is chew *qat*."

Sana'a is home away from home for Islam's political refugees, and its cafés are crawling with Iraqis, Iranians, Afghanis, and Somalis, all indulging in the favorite sport of expats worldwide, that of slagging off their host country. Ishamel had come to Sana'a with his father twenty years ago and now appeared completely assimilated. He even wore the *jambiya* dagger in his belt. The only things that gave him away as an Afghani were the hints of henna in his beard and a streak of larceny a mile wide.

I'd told him I was interested in how people first started drinking coffee. He told me a new version of the old goat story. There once was an Afghani goatherd with an unusually lively herd, he said. The goatherd couldn't understand why his flock was so frisky. One day he noticed that the liveliest of the goats were always nibbling on these little red berries. Curious, he tried a bean. His fatigue vanished. A sensuous tingly feeling crept across his thighs. He grabbed his prettiest she-goat and...

And so bestiality was discovered. It was the old Kaldi story, although the X-rated component was new.

"Right," I said. "And I guess that's why people think *qahwa* turns you into a demon lover?"

"No. But that is why Yemen men drink so much coffee," he winked. "They love their goats."

"And the shepherds of Afghan do not love their herds?" I teased.

"Not with such passion. Ask an Afghani if he prefers an English girl to a goat, and he will give you answer. Ask a Yemen man, and he will say, 'How to compare? I've never had an English.'"

"Yeah, yeah, yeah. I know that one. Tell me something new."

"You want hash?"

I declined. I did, however, need to change money. Doing it in Sana'a had proved a tad complicated. Not that the black market was hard to find. There was a whole street of young boys sitting on the pavement with piles of money until two or three in the morning, apparently without fear. It was just that no one had ever seen a traveler's check before. The one check I tried to change was accepted after a fierce debate among the crowd, only to be returned once I'd endorsed it because I was "writing on money and made it no good."

Ishmael said he knew a man who could not only change traveler's checks but also obtain European passports, something I was most definitely in the market for. We popped over. The electricity was out, as usual, so there was neither light nor fans. Traditionally dressed Yemen men squatted amid piles of rubbish, counting cash and sipping tea, their cheeks bulging with *qat*, while their wealthier Saudi customers strutted and tugged at the cuffs of their Western dinner jackets, the better to display their heavy gold watches. I handed a stranger my check, and it began a circuit of the room hand by hand. There was a burst of excitement, and the moneychanger snatched it away from one man and threw it into a box, only to immediately pull it back out, grab two huge stacks of bills, and pass the combo over to me, yelling I should sign. Nobody asked for my passport.

A man gestured I should sit on the floor next to him. I began to count, but there was not enough light to see the bills' value. My neighbor lit his cigarette lighter and began helping me tally the money, constantly stopping to exchange comments with any of the dozens of men that kept stepping over us. Another stack of notes was handed through the crowd and placed at my side. All this was done with the strange casual rhythm I'd come to associate with *qat*.

The money was fine. But it turned out Ishmael's moneychanger knew nothing about European passports.

"Talk to my other friend," Ishmael suggested before he headed out to "do business." He gestured to the stranger who'd been counting my money. Apparently he was the passport expert. Two nationalities were available—new Greek or used German.

I asked about price.

He shrugged. "As you like," he said. "You help me, I help you."

I was still straining to see what my new friend looked like, but all I could see in the darkened room was a head of henna-dyed hair. Another Afghani.

"Help?" I asked cautiously. "What kind of help?"

It seemed false passports were a sideline with him. His main business was smuggling political refugees to higher-paying countries. If I wanted a passport, I had to help him in a smuggling operation. I would have to fly to Frankfurt, with a stopover in Dubai. The refugee, who wanted to relocate to Germany, would get a ticket on the same flight. His ticket, however, would terminate in Dubai, and while on board we would exchange boarding passes. I would then disembark in Dubai while he, staying on the plane and using my pass, would continue on to Germany, thus avoiding having his passport being checked for a German visa. He would then destroy my ticket and all personal identification and present himself to the German authorities to claim asylum. Under the German constitution, he could not be turned away.

"And it is all true," the man assured me. "That is what is so beautiful about this lie. He is a refugee. In India."

"So he wants to work in Germany?"

"Of course! To help support his wife and children."

"Like you," I said, "I wish only to help. How much do I get paid?"

"Three hundred dollars."

Three hundred dollars, I thought. Not much. But an EEC passport would be quite handy.

"Plus the passport," I added. " Preferably French."

He nodded.

"And you pay for the tickets," I threw in.

"Of course. And a ticket to wherever you want to go after Dubai."

That was easy, I thought; there must be something wrong.

"What happens if I get caught?" I asked.

"Happens? What you mean?"

"By the police."

"Police? Why police? What is crime? You buy ticket, you give it to a friend." He shrugged. "We have a saying: *al-ibaha al-asliya*. 'If it is not forbidden, it is allowed.'"

Segue heaven! This was exactly the same argument that coffee lovers used in the early 1500s when religious bigots made having a cup of joe a crime. This might seem ridiculous, but one has to remember how closely associated coffee was with the mystical Sufi sect. Al-Shadhili of Mocha was a Sufi, as was al-Dhabhani in Aden, and, while Sufism is Islamic, it is so in the same way a whale is a mammal—just barely. Traditional Muslims use neither music nor dance in their ceremonies. Sufis use both. Sufism is an unusually heterogeneous religion, ostensibly Islamic but actually stemming from an earlier tradition. People have written volumes trying to explain it, but the best way to understand is via this old story told in the Middle East.

A Persian, a Turk, a Greek, and an Arab are discussing how to spend their last shekel.

"I want ouzo," cried the Greek.

"I want angur [wine]," argues the Persian.

The Arab and the Turk do the same, demanding wine in their own languages. A fight is about to break out. Just then a Sufi wanders by, listens, and asks that they give him their money. They do, and he soon returns with a bunch of glistening grapes.

"My ouzo!" cries the Greek.

"No—it's my angur!" says the Persian. Ditto for the Turk and the Arab. All are happy, for they have been given what they asked for, but in a higher sense.

In this parable wine represents the intoxication of God which Sufism seeks in its purest and most universal form. It also implies that the Sufis like an occasional drink. They're essentially the hippies of Islam, so, when the Sufis started using coffee in their religious ceremonies in the holy city of Mecca around 1480, it was a bit like lighting up a joint in the Vatican.

The first suppression of coffee began June 20, 1511, when

the head of Mecca's religious police, a Mamluk Muslim named Kha'ir Beg, noticed a group of men swallowing some drink "in the fashion of drinkers swallowing an intoxicant" late at night near the Holy Mosque. When he approached to investigate, the men extinguished their lanterns. Mr. Beg soon learned that the men had been drinking *qahwa*, a drink that he was told was consumed in places similar to taverns.

The next day he convened a hearing of religious scholars to decide whether this new drink was legal under Islamic law. The official objections to coffee were threefold. One, it was an intoxicant and so, like wine, forbidden. Two, the Sufis' preprayer cup of joe was passed hand to hand, an act also associated with drinking alcohol. Three, it was roasted to the point of "carbonization," a process forbidden in the Koran. Islamic law, *Shari'a*, is essentially the Koran, which specifically forbids alcoholic fermented drinks. Coffee was clearly not a fermented fruit beverage, so the zealots at the hearing claimed it was illegal because "it excites the mind." A pot of coffee was brought in so the judges could try it for themselves. This, of course, was much too simple for this bunch of Poindexters, all of whom refused to sample the devilish brew.

Mr. Beg had apparently foreseen this and brought out two doctors to testify to the drink's horrific effects, according to the eighteenth-century manuscript *Chrestonathic Arabe*. Here the plot thickens, for, reported a contemporary, the two doctors were actually in cahoots with Mr. Beg and had promised him "great glory and rewards" if he could get coffee banned. Big surprise, they testified that coffee caused mental alterations in the drinker and was therefore a type of "wine." Others at the hearing claimed that coffee clouded their judgment. One fool even said he found it indistinguishable from wine, only to be promptly whipped for confessing he had tasted alcohol.

The argument for keeping coffee legal was the same that my Afghani passport counterfeiter gave—*al-ibaha al-asliya*, a Hanafi principle of Islamic jurisprudence which stipulates that whatever is not explicitly forbidden in the Koran is allowed. When the conservatives argued that Mohammed had meant to ban all intoxicants, coffee lovers pointed out that, although the cup did have psychological effects, so did garlic, and that the traditional Islamic definition of intoxication was "when one is incapable of distinguishing man from woman, or heaven from earth."

The whole trial was a staged event with a political agenda. Mr. Beg and the two doctors were part of the ruling conservative Mamluk coalition, which frowned on the Sufi belief in a religious ecstasy, or "intoxication," during which there is one-to-one communication with God. The Sufis' use of coffee as an intoxicant epitomized this thinking. The drink was passed hand to hand from their *sheykah*, or priest, thus symbolizing its role as a sanctified intoxicant. The Sufis even had a term for the religious high associated with coffee, *marqaha*. The implication that there was no need for an imam—a cleric—or a mosque, did not sit well with the authorities.

Coffee was banned throughout Mecca. Bags of beans were burned in the streets, and anybody found drinking it was beaten on the spot. The ban was later scuttled, only to be reinstated in Mecca in 1525 and Cairo in 1539, with each suppression growing increasingly violent, until the vicious Turkish suppression of the 1600s.

Of course, I wasn't sure whether medieval Islamic jurisprudence would carry much weight with Interpol if they caught me smuggling refugees across international borders. But it was something to think about.

Java

He who drinks only a little* qahwa, *he will not go to Hell.

Sixteenth-century Sufi saying

THE BAFFLING LACK OF JAVA that had plagued me on my first day in Sana'a continued throughout my stay. Lots of stalls, simple huts manned by maniacal Arabs, but not much coffee, or at least what I'd thought of as Arabic joe. I'd expected something along the lines of Turkish coffee, strong and muddy. But a cup of Yemen is a different fish. Here the coffee, while strong and clear, is only one flavor in a delicate mélange of cloves, cardamom, sugar, and water. It strikes the Western palate as rather pallid at first, but I came to love its fragrant delicacy. It is made in two ways. One is called *shatter*, made by steeping a heaping tablespoon of spiced, ground coffee in hot water. This is generally favored in the afternoon. In the mornings sugar and coffee are boiled together in the long-handled pot, called the *ibrik*, and served piping hot. The resulting concoction is, however, far removed from the traditional Turkish brew, a difference that illustrates the nations' contrasting temperaments. Turkish coffee is like a clenched fist in a cup—tight, bitter, and black. The Yemen version, which comes glowing golden in a large glass tumbler, is a lighter, more whimsical brew, and deliciously sweet (except at funerals, at which the addition of sugar is forbidden). Milk is rarely used.

Instead of coffee, many Yemenites drink *qisher*, a beverage brewed from the husk of the coffee bean instead of the seed. This is the historic coffee drink of Yemen. "*People of distinction have another method that does not use the bean, but the bark and flesh,*" wrote Jean de La Roque in 1715. "*When well prepared they claim that no other beverage is comparable.*"

The apparent line of development, from Ethiopia's leaf-based *kati* to *qisher*, has caused some to speculate that our modern bean-based brew evolved because these earlier bases were too perishable to transport. I found *qisher* rather dull, although drinkable when flavored with ginger, when it is called *mazghoul*. The closest thing we have to it in the West is a German ordeal called *blumchenkaffee*, "flower cup," because it is so weak one can see the floral design on the bottom of the mug.

"Ahh, but you must have good *qisher*," said Ibraham. He gestured dismissively to the cup before me. "This is just made by my boys. Young people have lost the art."

We were seated on floor cushions scattered about his *muffraj*, the top-floor room reserved for entertaining guests in traditional Yemeni homes. Ibraham's *muffraj*, however, was on the ground floor and boasted a satellite TV, since he'd recently turned his home into a hotel.

It was my third visit. He described to me again the traditional method of brewing, which can involve up to a dozen different pots of *qisher*, some bitter, some sweet, some long brewed, which are then blended carefully to create the perfect cup. There was one family, he said, whose women were renowned throughout Yemen for their *qisher*. I asked if I could perhaps meet them. Unthinkable, he said. A woman of Sana'a show a foreign man how to cook *qisher*? Well then, I asked, could he get me the recipe? Equally inconceivable. Just their names, maybe? Everything was impossible. But there was a café he knew that had good *qisher*. Nothing as exquisitely mind-bending as this family's. Ahh, that was *qisher*! But good, good enough for a foreigner.

"Once you have had it, you will see," he said. He gave me directions to this legendary café one more time. Again he drew the map, as he had on the other two occasions, neither of which had helped me to find the place.

"You, I think, will never find it," he concluded.

"Why don't you take me there?" I begged.

"Impossible." He gestured to the TV. "Today is busy day. Tomorrow."

"Well, then tell me the name of a place I can find."

This called for a conference with a friend in Arabic. Ibraham suddenly slapped himself on the head.

"Of course! My friend knows," he said. "You must look for the old men."

"What?"

"Go in the morning after first prayer and look around the mosques. Wherever you see lots of old men drinking, there you'll find the best *qisher*."

Look for the Sign of the Old Men, I thought. Near the mosques. Made sense. After all, cafés grew up around mosques so the faithful could stay conscious during services.

"The best is made after first prayer," he said. "Remember, the older the men, the better the *qisher*."

"What time is first prayer anyhow?"

"Not so early. Maybe five A.M."

Five in the morning! Was it worth it? And why after prayer? If cafés had developed as a way of keeping the faithful conscious for the Word for God, why was everybody drinking in them *after* services? This, I was told, was the final compromise in the Islamic campaign against coffee, at least in Yemen. The faithful were to refrain from getting wired until after the first morning prayer, thus allowing the Word of the Prophet to reach their hearts unpolluted by devilish stimulants. And if you had to have a cup first thing, you should do as they did in Istanbul during the 1600s, crying out as you downed the brew, "Soul, retire into some corner of my body or leave but for a while that you may not be contaminated by this substance."

That's the story I was told. And it was true that there was a noticeable difference between the *qahwa* served in the morning and in the afternoon. Those morning cups were a good fur-raising jolt. In the afternoon, when most people were chewing *qat*, the light brew, *shatter*, was poured. Most drank *qisher*.

THE PASSPORT SCHEME WAS EVAPORATING. IT TURNED OUT THAT I actually first had to fly to Sri Lanka to meet the refugee. There, another Afghani, who owned a travel agency, would supply me with the tickets for Dubai. I was beginning to get the picture, and it looked suspiciously like me sitting in the most terrorist-infested city in the world for a few weeks while someone's cousin, or friend's cousin, or friend's cousin's friend's cousin, hunted around for cheap tickets. Oh, it would happen. Eventually. *Bismillah*.

"I have to get out of this country," said Gulab. "I go crazy."

Gulab was an Iraqi archeology professor turned draft dodger who I'd met at the café where I ate bean sandwiches, *foul*, for breakfast. Like most of the refugees I met here, he hated Yemen; the people were too backward, too dirty, the food was awful. Blah, blah, blah. I thought everyone was supernice and the food quite tasty. The environs safe. I walked about the winding, unlit alleys of the old city until the wee hours of the morning without a worry (perhaps because criminals are still crucified here). Unfortunately for Gulab, Yemen was one of the few countries still granting visas to Iraqis in the aftermath of the Gulf War. The other two were Romania and Libya. Libya was fine with Gulab, lots of oil-rig work, but no international airline would land there since Khadaffi had refused to cooperate in the Lockerbie bombing investigation. So Gulab had been obliged to come to Yemen or Romania, or be drafted. He'd chosen Yemen because he'd heard its Sudanese embassy sometimes granted Iraqis transit visas. This would allow him to land in Khartoum, from which point he could theoretically *walk* to Libya, albeit through some of the most war-torn real estate around. It was a popular route for peace-loving Iraqis. He personally knew several other academics who had mysteriously disappeared while making the trek.

He was definitely in a tough spot. I tried to cheer him up by telling him that the Sudanese people were renowned for their hospitality. I even showed him the page in my guidebook where it said so. But he was inconsolable. He just kept saying how he would "go crazy" if I didn't help him get out. Word was out that I ran an international refugee-placement service.

"It's so dirty I can't believe," he kept nagging as he followed me about the old quarter. "If I have to stay I go crazy."

I soon eluded him. The electricity was out, as it was every night, but the *suq* continued by candlelight. Silversmiths polished curved daggers, men made water pipes. Everywhere there were piles of myrrh and incense. As I wandered through the claustrophobic alleys, I thought about my impending journey along the coffee trail. Once purchased in Mocha or Bay al-Faqih, most beans were brought by boat to Jedda in Saudi Arabia. Some think, however, that the earliest shipments went via the ancient spice routes through the famous desert landscapes of the Empty Quarter, and hence to Mecca. I had to decide which of the two routes I should, or could, follow.

Suddenly I heard a roar of excitement. The electricity had returned. Literally every window in Old Sana'a is made of stained glass, with up to forty windows in a single building. The effect, on those rare nights when the electricity worked, was magical. I unexpectedly stumbled upon one of the city's open gardens. The starry sky sprang open above me, and everywhere I looked were the ghostly mud skyscrapers, their windows glittering like jewels, all green and red and blue and amber. Prayer calls swirled out from every alley.

I decided to follow the spice routes through the Empty Quarter.

My plans changed the next day when I found a postcard waiting for me at Sana'a's central post office. It was from Yangi, a Rajasthani art forger I'd met in Calcutta. "Remember," his message read. "We shall always be friends of the heart. Paris waits."

I moaned out loud. It seemed our "business" was still operative. Unless I pretended the letter had never arrived; probably the wisest thing to do. Yangi, Yangi, Yangi, I thought, tossing out the postcard. Damn him! Despite all the bullshit, despite all the trouble he had caused me, I still had a soft spot for the bastard.

Monkey Droppings

One need only compare the violent coffee-drinking societies of the West to the peace-loving tea drinker of the Orient to realize the pernicious and malignant effect that bitter brew has upon the human soul.

Hindi dietary tract, anonymous

I'D FIRST MET YANGI FOUR months earlier in a cavernous old coffeehouse in Calcutta. I remember it all quite clearly; the waiters in their white turbans, the socialist posters, the sea of slowly spinning fans heavy with clumped filth. On one wall hung an oil portrait of the poet R. Tagore. He'd been a regular customer when he won his Nobel fifty years ago and seemed still to provide a role model for the students who packed the place—fat, whiskery fellows munching samosas and slurping chai, girls with blue jeans under their saris. Calcutta's progressive wing. The day I met Yangi even the balcony tables were full, and the crowd's roar was so loud that people leaning over the railing to shriek out their order were inaudible; only the writhing of their lips could be seen, and their faces, distorted by the intervening sea of whirling ceiling fans, looked like shimmering gargoyles.

Yangi was sitting alone at a corner table. Beautiful man—luminous, almond-shaped eyes, dreamy lips, flawless caramel skin, long jet-black hair. He rolled a cigarette. He sighed. When I later found out what a *bhang* (hash) fiend he was, his behavior made perfect sense. At the time I was puzzled how anybody could find staring at an unlit cigarette for forty-five minutes so amusing. No one tried to sit at his table, or speak to him. As I left, he looked up and gave me a sleepy smile. He was cross-eyed.

I was working for Mother Teresa at the time, handfeeding emaciated men one day, carrying out their corpses the next, and this café was my favorite hangout. Most people do not understand why I love Calcutta. Think of it as Paris circa 1930—cheap, dirty, and full of poorly washed people sitting about babbling nonsense. Like Paris in its heyday, Calcutta is its nation's intellectual capital, and this particular café is probably the heart of it all. Two of India's three Nobel Prize winners frequented the joint, and even its name, the Indian Coffeeworkers Union Syndicate, is quintessential Calcutta; the owner had become so involved in the political ramifications of a café that he'd neglected to indicate that coffee was served on the premises. Nevertheless, the place is perpetually packed, and when next I visited, it was once again full. Likewise, Yangi was sitting alone. He waved me over.

"Sit," he said. "All the tables are taken."

He asked me what I thought of Calcutta. I said it was dirty

but interesting.

"So dirty!" he agreed. "And the Bengalese—they talk so much! Talk, talk, talk, talk!"

He spoke with a languid drawl. His eyes seemed permanently half-closed.

"You are not Bengali?" I asked.

"No. Me? Himal Pradesh."

"Strange. You look like you are Bengali."

"Yes," he drawled, giving me a dopey look. "I look like Bengal." There was a pause while I tried to figure that one out. He pointed to a painting on a nearby wall. "You know this man?"

It was the portrait of Tagore. Yes, I said, I knew him. I told Yangi that the café had also been the headquarters for the Calcutta clique of the revolt against the British, a pro-violence wing whose leader, Subhas Chandra Bose, eventually allied himself with the Nazis. I mentioned how the café's manager had refused to talk about this bit of history without a contribution for the "charity fund," then denied it had ever happened. "No politics in the coffeehouse," he'd said. "Only artists."

"Charity fund—ha!" sneered Yangi when I told him. "Managers are all liars. The Bengal only do politics. Everything is political. Politics! Politics! Politics! Talk! Talk! Talk!"

"You don't like Bengalis?"

"Oh no. They are fine." He fell back in his chair, apparently exhausted by his little outburst. "Only I don't care about politics, Stewart. Bullshit. I like money."

"Useful stuff."

"Ha-ha! Stuff!" He gave the table a languid smack. "I like you. You are a funny man." He leaned toward me conspiratorially. His breath was spicy and sweet. "Maybe you like we get rich together. Hmm?"

THE CAFÉ-AS-A-PLACE-OF-CONSPIRACY WAS THE INSTITUTION'S first incarnation as it evolved away from its religious roots. The vast majority of the conspiracies were political. But the type of financial conspiracy that Yangi was about to propose also has a long history, with a particularly rich chapter belonging to the seventeenth-century English coffeehouse.

Once upon a time many years ago, while most of continental Europe still believed coffee dried up one's brain cells, London was the café capital of the world. This was about 1680. There was one particular establishment, Lloyd's Coffeehouse, where sea captains and merchants met to hear the latest shipping news. Boats went down on a regular basis back then, and when they did, their owners were out of luck. One day some of Lloyd's regulars started offering odds on which ships would make it to port. If an owner's ship stayed afloat, he lost the bet and Lloyd's kept his money; if it went down, the boys at Lloyd's had to pay for the loss. According to insurance historian F. H. Haines, "Coffeehouses like Lloyd's provided a place where ideas were developed as they would never have been in the private guildhalls and brain muddled tap rooms."

Lloyd's was not the first instance of insurance, but it was the first modern manifestation. With the risk removed, shipping took off, and Britain soon had the world's largest merchant marine. The fellows who hung out at the Jerusalem Café also did quite well, and their company, the East India Company, was soon the largest shipping conglomerate in the world.

Lloyd's Coffeehouse, however, did not prosper. With all the comings and goings, and merchants making their stalls into little offices, the café had to give up serving coffee altogether and settle for being the world's largest insurance firm, Lloyd's of London, Ltd.

Yangi's "business" scheme, which unfolded over several

weeks, was a tad more modest. He had an artist friend in the northwest province of Rajasthan who was painting a group of fake antique Mogol paintings for a show in Paris. The problem was that for the paintings to be sold as antiques, they needed official papers, which meant a huge export tax. Foreigners, however, could take antiques out of the country at a much lower tax rate if they were purchased as presents. If I were willing to take some of his friend's forged antique paintings to Paris "as presents," and then hand them over in time for the upcoming show, they would pay me three thousand dollars.

I loved the concept of art smuggling and forgery, so pretty and tricky. I also quite liked the Rajasthani school of miniatures: jewel-like paintings incorporating gold leaf and fantastical animals. The catch was, I didn't believe a word Yangi said.

"When do you think you get to Paris?" he asked, after outlining the scheme.

"Maybe February."

He slammed his hand on the table. "Perfect!"

What a surprise, I thought. It's all falling into place.

"So would you want to do this?" he asked. "It would be such a favor to my friend..."

"Hmm...It is illegal."

"Yes but no. You will be selling the paintings. They are yours to sell, yes?"

"But that implies that I bought them. This means I have to give you money."

Yangi waved the possibility away. "No, no. I don't know. They may want you to pay for the insurance. That is only reasonable. You will have all the paintings." He gave me a blissful smile. "So beautiful. Little jewels. When do you arrive to Rajasthan?"

"Around November."

He wrote down directions to a café in the so-called Pink City of Jaipur. "Ask for me here. Then you will decide."

I hadn't been planning to visit Jaipur. But I didn't want to kill the whole scheme. The idea of being an international art smuggler was terrifically romantic. And three thousand dollars would be useful.

"I don't know..."

"No problem!" he drawled, pushing the directions into my hands. "As you like. If you are in Jaipur, come. You will like Jaipur," he whispered. "The Pink City!"

MOST PEOPLE DO NOT ASSOCIATE INDIA WITH COFFEE. DISORGANized, dirty, undereducated, lazy, muddled, poor, and run-down—not to mention superstitious—it is clearly a nation of tea drinkers. But, in fact, India was the first non-Muslim nation to have our beloved plant take root in its soil. This was thanks to an Indian Sufi named Baba Budan. Baba means papa, but his real name was Hazrat Shah Jamer Allah Mazarabi. Some time ago, nobody knows when, Baba made the pilgrimage to Mecca, where he met Sufis using coffee in their rituals. Baba naturally decided he should bring this wonderful substance back to his home in south-central India to share with his Sufi brothers. Taking live coffee beans out of Mecca, however, was punishable by beheading. So first Mr. B. did the Mecca thing. He revolved around the Holy Kaaba seven times. He kissed the Black Stone. He drank from the holy Zam-Zam. Then he taped seven green coffee beans to his belly and smuggled them back to India to plant high in the mountains near Mysore. These seeds gave birth to today's two-hundred-thousand-ton a year industry, as well as providing the seedling that the Dutchman Captain Adrian Van Ommeren used to found Indonesia's great coffee plantations in 1696.[1]

Since I knew so little about Baba, I headed south from Calcutta toward his home in the mountains near Mysore. It's a thousand-mile journey, five days by train, and as I meandered down the rails, it was interesting to note the differences between the coffee-loving south and the tea-drinking north. Northern train stations were filthy, filled with homeless families and reeking of urine. An endless parade of beggars cruised the aisles. As we reached the southern states, the beggars became rarer, stations were cleaner, and schedules were sometimes adhered to. People looked healthier, as well they might, since coffee consumption, literacy, and income levels were about twice as high as in the north.

The method of service on the trains also offered an interesting peek at what's to come as the world's second largest nation modernizes. Tea and coffee vendors have traditionally served their brews in rough clay pots, which you smash underfoot when done. Good fun, hygienic, and completely biodegradable. With the entry of entities like Nescafé, these traditional vessels are gradually being replaced by shot-size plastic cups. I asked one vendor what he thought would happen when India Rail's three billion annual customers had all switched to plastic. Did he think there might be a little littering problem?

"Problem? No problem!" He pointed to a beggar collecting discarded plastic cups and placing them in a filthy bag. I looked at the cup in my hand. So much for the illusion of hygiene, I thought. "You see," he continued proudly, "Indians are very good at recycling."

MYSORE PROVED TO BE A PLEASANTLY COOL CITY WITH WIDE, shady streets and not too much traffic. We loved it. (I say "we" because I was traveling with my lover, Nina, who is too modest

[1] A number of coffee historians believe it was the Dutch who first brought the bean to India around 1680. However, the British *Journal of Mythic Society VII* claims that in A.D. 1385 Emperor Harihara II of Vijayanagar (now Mysore) ordered that all imports for Peta Math enter tax free in "return for coffee seeds." This certainly puts the Dutch claim to primacy in doubt.

to appear in these pages.) I'd soon heard the usual range of misinformation. Baba, I was told, was a Muslim saint. No, he was a Hindu deity. He was renowned for his generosity. He trained his pet tigers to milk cows. He had a troop of wild monkeys that picked his coffee beans. There was a university named after him.

"University? Tigers? This is nonsense," said Mr. Chaterjee. "There is only the temple in Chickmagalur, and to tell you truthfully, it is a disgrace. Best not to go."

Mr. Chaterjee, whom I met at a Mysore café, looked a bit like an educated parrot. But he seemed to know what was what. According to him, there was an active shrine to Baba Budan about two hundred miles away. As this was India, it was of course more complicated, for although there was a Baba shrine where Muslims prayed, the same spot, a cave, was also a shrine to a Hindu deity called Dattatreya, who had at some point entered the cave and was expected to come back out at the beginning of the new millennium.

"But I tell you, it is a disgrace to the Indian people," warned Chaterjee. "I beg of you not to go."

The problem lay in Baba's habit of giving his clothes to beggars, a tradition his followers continued by first bathing in a holy waterfall and then leaving their clothes hanging on tree branches for the destitute. Unfortunately, devotees performed the ceremony in such tattered rags that even the poorest of the poor wouldn't touch them, and the forest around the shrine was now festooned with an ocean of rotten, fly-infested clothing, according to Chaterjee.

"I even have a letter that I took from the *Deccan Herald* on the subject." Chaterjee pulled a clipping out of his oversized briefcase. "Look—my friend has written demanding rectification. But there is no satisfaction."

His newspaper clipping demanded that "authorities clean up

this holy place" and make it into an official site.

"So this is an issue here?" I asked.

"Not for everyone, perhaps. But Baba was a great holy man."

Chaterjee told me that he had once been in the coffee business down by a place called Shrevenoot.

"Excellent coffee. You know of course that Karnataka grows the best coffee beans in the world?"

"I'd heard," I replied politely. "I must say, though, I find the coffee here a little milky."

"Well, milk is another matter entirely."

I let it pass and asked instead about some of the stories I'd heard.

"Do you know anything about how Baba trained his tigers to milk cows?"

"That is just mythology."

"Like the monkeys, I suppose."

"I know no monkeys."

"You haven't heard how he trained his monkeys to pick the beans for him?"

"More nonsense." He took a sip of his tea. "There are, of course, the coffee-picking monkeys of Shrevenoot."

I laughed. "Wait—so there are actually monkeys trained to pick coffee beans?"

"Of course not. They are not trained. It is a natural phenomenon. They pick the fruit off the tree and eat. That is how you get Monkey Coffee. Surely you have heard?"

Actually, I had read about this stuff. Monkey Coffee was something that had existed in the nineteenth century, supposedly the best brew in the world.

"So there really is such a thing?" I asked.

"It is a well-known fact. I have read it is a delicacy in some countries."

"Yes, yes. I've read that too. They say it is because the monkeys will pick only the best, the ripest berries, right?"

"So some say. Others claim it is the chemical reaction within the bowels."

"Bowels?"

"Yes. The monkeys eat the beans and then pass them through their digestive system. That is the monkey coffee."

"You mean it's monkey, uh, feces?"

"As I have said, nobody drinks it here. They are unclean animals." He wrinkled his nose. "But it was a terrible problem in Shrevenoot. The monkeys ate all the best beans."

I was never quite sure whether to believe all this until much later, back in the States, when I discovered that Monkey Coffee had recently become part of the gourmet coffee roster. It does not, however come out of either a monkey or India, but a small Indonesian creature called the palm toddy cat,[2] a nocturnal tree lover that lives on the naturally alcoholic tree sap used to make palm toddy (wine), and fresh coffee berries. Whether it's because the animal's intestinal juices impart some special flavor (perhaps because of its alcoholic diet) or merely because it eats only perfectly ripe berries, the toddy cat's droppings, cleaned, produce what many say is the world's finest coffee. Japan buys most of the stuff nowadays, but the U.S. firm of M. P. Mountanos (800-229-1611) sells it under the name Kopi Luwak at about three hundred dollars a pound, making it the world's most expensive cup of joe. Another firm, called Raven's Brew Coffee (ravencup@ptialaska.net or 800-91-RAVEN), sells it by the quarter pound for seventy-five dollars and, in that grand American tradition, throws in a free T-shirt showing the beast

[2] Some Ethiopians credit the civet cat, which produces musk from a gland near its rectum, with spreading coffee via its droppings.

hard at work with a cup under its ass and the caption "Good to the Last Dropping."

THE DUBIOUS PLEASURES OF MONKEY COFFEE ASIDE, INDIA produces the world's most consistently vile cup of joe. It is never fresh-brewed but made with instant "flakes," which are boiled with milk, sugar, and nutmeg. The resulting stew is best described as a sickeningly sweet, piping-hot milkshake, the memory of which is a dark blot upon my soul. The whole thing is not only vile, it's illogical. Tropical cuisines worldwide avoid dairy products like the plague. Here they were worshiped. How could a culture with such fine cuisine be content with such a perversion? I just couldn't understand.

One day, as I walked down a lonely desert road near the city of Jodhpur, I was given my answer.

"COME, FRIEND," SAID A VOICE. "COME DRINK WITH ME."

I hadn't noticed the little house by the side of the highway

"Come!" There was a man sitting on the porch, gesturing I should sit beside him. "Tea!"

"What is the price?" I asked.

"Oh, there is no price here. Free! Come, come sit." He pointed to a stool at his feet. "This has been saved for you."

He was a fat man with a happy face. Wisps of beard trickled down his shirt front. I sat.

He told me that his house contained eighty-three steel jugs filled with water.

"The metal," he said, "keeps the liquid cool in even the fiercest heat, the better to quench the thirst of strangers such as yourself."

This, he said, was his *geas*, his duty, as it had been his father's before him, to ease the thirst of any stranger who might pass, at no cost.

"There are only three things man needs for life," he explained. "Air, water, and food. Is it not wonderful that God has provided the first, the most important, air, at no charge?"

My memory of that day seems terribly unreal. I remember the flies that dotted his beard like jewels, crawling up his robe, quivering on the brim of my teacup. I remember the filth. My teacup was disgusting, covered with black-stained cracks, sticky to the touch. And I remember that, despite this, I drank.

Then he mentioned Lord Krishna.

"It is this third essential, food, that we spend all our days running here and there for. And why? Because our teeth are flat." He smiled down at me. "You see? For we are not flesh eaters but should follow the example of Lord Krishna and enjoy our days on this earth eating of the fruit and vegetables nature provides, and drinking of the milk from the cows that wander here and there."

Krishna is the name those orange people at the airports are always chanting, a fun loving, flirtatious god fond of good food, particularly milk or cream or sweet butter. As a child he was constantly making himself ill by drinking fifteen gallons of cream in one sitting. As he matured, he began preaching a creed of universal love in long, intricately rhymed sermons. But the cow still held a special place in his heart. Cows, he taught, are beautiful. They are of the sweetest disposition. Their milk is full of vitamins. Treated with love, it becomes butter or cream or curd. Their excrement, properly dried, makes excellent fuel for cooking. In short, a cow's orifices are veritable fountains of delight, providing all of life's necessities, and anything it drips, drops, or drools is good for both body and karma.

I finally understood the Indian cup. Every religion has its sacred brew. Christians and Jews have wine; Buddhists, tea (said to have grown from Siddhartha's eyelash); Muslims, coffee. For Hindus it is milk from the sacred cow. All that had puzzled me was now made clear: the man who had criticized a coffeemaker for "putting water in his milk;" the huge vats of reducing cream used to make "special" coffee; the puzzled looks of vendors when I had asked for my cup black.

Every foreigner in India has his or her moment of enlightenment. This was mine. He was my guru.

"And so, Baba," I said, "that is why the Indian puts too much milk in his coffee?"

"Yes, my son." He clicked his tongue disapprovingly. "But you should drink only tea. Coffee is a bitter liquid that produces a rumbling of the bowels."

Mother Calcutta

"He was perpetually 'going Fantee' among the natives, which of course no man with any sense believes in."
(*Plain Tales from the Hills*, "Miss Youghal Sais")

When Rudyard Kipling wrote that line in 1886, "going native" (or Fantee) meant that an Englishman had taken to wearing pajamas in public. The first warning that I was going native was my "enlightenment" near Jodhpur. The next was a growing desire to buy a pair of purple polyester slacks. They're quite common in India, and though I struggled against the impulse, I finally succumbed in Bikaneer, a Rajasthani town where live rats are worshiped. Now, there is no excuse for such aberrant shopping. In my defense I can only point out that my lover, Nina, who normally guides me through the treacherous morass of high fashion, had returned to the United States. Furthermore, disease had reduced me to a shadow of my former self. I'd lost forty pounds, almost a third of my normal weight, leaving both my body and mind weakened. It's a common condition among travelers hereabouts, and no doubt accounts for the number of Westerners who get religion while in India.

Fortunately my conversion was limited to couture. I thought myself quite chic as I swept into Jaipur in my luminous pantaloons, filthy sandals, and a straw hat that was now a mass of dusty leather patches.

"Nice pants," was Yangi's first comment. "You've really got a look now."

After introducing me to an acne-scarred Sikh named Happy, he led me into a maze of alleys through which we wandered until we came to a two-foot-tall door. We crawled through and into a long, empty room with another midget door at the other end. We squeezed through this and found ourselves in his friend's art studio, a windowless chamber covered with brilliantly colored Rajasthani miniatures depicting talking rats and elephant-headed gods. It was like finding a ruby in a pile of dung, all gold leaf and electric reds that glittered in the candlelight. I loved it.

The basic premise, as I have mentioned, was that I would carry these "antique" paintings (forgeries) to Paris, where, for a fee, I would deliver them to the artist in time for his show, thus avoiding taxation on antiques.

Business in that part of the world is a long-winded, intricate, and illogical affair. So I won't go into details, like my meeting with the English traveler who had done a similar deal. Or the bizarre ceremony at the Ape God's temple and the coconut shell of friendship. I shall also pass lightly over my meeting with an "official" underwriting the transaction.

Rather, let us skip to three days later, when I found myself in a dusty back-alley shop signing twelve hundred dollars' worth of credit card slips for a package of paintings, the actual contents of which I'd never even seen. We then mailed the package to me care of Paris's central post office.

"You must get there by February," warned Yangi as we parted company. "I will see you in Delhi tomorrow."

Some of my most vivid memories of India are of simple rickshaw rides like the one I took that day—the porters carrying ten-foot-tall bundles on their heads, the donkey carts and lowing bulls, the lunatic tuk-tuks (three-wheeled motorbikes) and occasional elephant. My ride to the train station that day proved particularly memorable because, as we neared the station, a motor scooter carrying two Sikhs zipped out of the chaos and rode parallel with my bicycle rickshaw.

"You, you," shouted the fat Sikh on the back. "American, you know me?"

"Do I?" I yelled. Since all Sikhs wear the same turban, prescribed by their religion, I'm always thinking I just met them.

"We met in the café—Yangi's friend!" I had met some Sikhs via Yangi. "You gave him money, yes?"

At the word *money* my driver looked back to see what was going on.

"Maybe."

"I'm sorry, but you will never see your money again," shouted the Sikh. "I wanted to warn you."

We all swerved to the right. An elephant stacked with palm leaves lumbered past. I controlled the urge to throw up.

"Thanks!" I screamed. "Bit late now, don't you think?"

He shrugged. "He's an old friend." A swarm of black and yellow tuk-tuks buzzed past. "How much did you give him?"

"Too much," I yelled. "Leave me alone."

He grinned and zoomed off into the traffic. I immediately directed my driver to a telephone center, where I tried to cancel the payment. This, of course, was not allowed. Then, in a moment of self-fury, I tore up my credit card. I was obviously too stupid to be entrusted with one. During the four-hour train ride to Delhi I went through a hundred schemes to get my money back. But they had me. There was no way to reach Yangi, or cancel the payment. After the maze of alleys they'd taken me through, I didn't even know how to find the painter or the shop where I'd used my card. I'd never felt so stupid. Idiot! I kept chanting in my head, dumbdumbdumbdumb. The outskirts of Delhi began to flicker past outside my window; mud huts plastered with dried cow dung, children in rags, putrescent pools of black water. I noticed that my reflection in the window was smiling. I'd had an idea.

I spent the next day waiting in the café where Yangi had arranged to meet me. When he failed to show I sought consolation in my tattered copy of a P. G. Wodehouse *Jeeves, Superbutler*. Around page 89, I looked up to find Yangi was sitting at my table.

"I knew I'd find you here," he drawled.

For a second I hesitated. Did I dare to go through with my scheme? Then I sprang out of my chair.

"Yangi!" I said, as if furious. "What the hell is going on?"

"What? I am late. We had problems with the car."

"Really? And would you like to tell me why the police were waiting for me at my hotel last night?" I hissed. "Do you have any idea?"

"Police? What police?"

"You mean you know nothing about it?"

"Know?" He looked mortified. "No, no..."

My story went like this. No sooner had I checked into my

Delhi hotel than five police officers dragged me off to the nearest station, where they questioned me all night about my "activities" in Jaipur. Had I bought anything there? Did I have any Sikh friends in Jaipur? Had I mailed any packets out of India in the last week? The questioning, I told Yangi, had continued until two in the morning.

Yangi was stunned.

"What did you tell them?"

"Nothing, nothing—but they kept asking about taxes."

"Taxes?"

"Yes." I lowered my voice. "And drugs."

"Drugs?" His eyes widened. "But why would they ask about drugs?"

"How should I know? But you have to tell me—were there any drugs in that package?"

"No, no drugs! No drugs!" He moaned. "This is crazy!"

"Because," I continued, "I protected you—I denied everything—but if there were any drugs in there..."

"No, no. You saw..."

"No. Remember, I never looked in the package." I had a sudden idea. "Did you pack the paintings in the box yourself?"

"No, not me. The painter's assistant packed them." He looked ill. "Could he...but no, this is crazy. There were no...no drugs."

"Because the police kept talking about heroin from Pakistan." Jaipur was renowned as a clearinghouse for the stuff.

"Heroin?"

"Could someone else have put heroin in the box?" I acted as if it were a foregone conclusion now. "And how did the police know my hotel? Only you and Happy knew where I was staying."

"No, no, no. " He put his head in his hands. "I don't understand how this could be happening..."

I prattled on for a bit. Yangi seemed stunned.

"Look," I said finally. "There should be no problem. As long as there aren't any drugs." I put my hand on his shoulder and looked deep into his eyes. "You swear there were no drugs?"

"Yes, yes, yes..."

"No heroin?"

"Nothing, nothing!"

"Then there should be no problem. They can't prove anything. I gave them no names." He looked relieved. Then I snapped my fingers as if I'd remembered something. "Oh, no..."

"What?"

"I didn't use my credit card to pay, did I?"

"Yes, with the card..."

"Hmmm. They took my card number down." I frowned. "Do you think they can trace it?"

"I don't know..."

"That could be a problem."

"But there is no crime in using your credit card."

"Yes. Except I told them I didn't buy anything in Jaipur. Now they'll know I lied." I shook my head uneasily. "If only I'd paid in cash." I paused. "You've put the slips through, of course?"

"Yes, this morning."

"Too bad. If we could have gotten them back I could just give you cash instead."

Yangi's ears perked up. "Cash?"

Within minutes he was on his way back to Jaipur to try to cancel the credit slips. Successful or not, he would meet me here day after next. Before he headed off, he made one last suggestion.

"Maybe is better if you just leave India, Stewart." He put his hand over mine comfortingly. "Maybe safer for you."

"I can't," I said in mock despair. "The police took my passport."

My plan (obviously) was to get the slips back, destroy them and take the first plane out of India. The problem was I had almost no cash and, having destroyed my credit card, I couldn't pay for the ticket.

For the next two days I tramped about Delhi trying to find a way to get some foreign currency. There was one particular street I walked up dozens of times in which lay a man, horribly emaciated, covered in flies. He was dying, of course; I knew that look all too well from working at Mother Teresa's. But along with thousands of other people, I did nothing. All I cared about was my money.

Yangi and I had arranged to meet at the Wimpy hamburger restaurant in Connaught Place. This time he arrived right on time. But he was not alone. Happy was in tow, as well as a muscle-bound "friend" I'd never met. They said the payment had already gone through and there was no way to get it back. Then they began interrogating me. They wanted to know exactly what questions the police had asked, what station we'd gone to, and what kind of uniform the officers had worn. I could tell that Yangi no longer believed my story. I lied lavishly, inventing outright, blending in half-truths. I even upped the ante by claiming the cops had visited me again with more questions. As proof, I produced a forged document showing that my credit card had been canceled by the police.

The boys were baffled.

"But why would they do this?"

"How should I know?" I asked. Then I produced my passport. "But at least they gave me my passport back."

The lies and counterlies went on for over an hour. They demanded I go with them to the police station; I refused until they found me a lawyer. They claimed to have one; I demanded to meet him.

Finally the interrogation ended. There was pause, and Happy pulled an envelope out of his pocket.

"We want to show you something." He pulled out the credit card slips.

"So the credit card charges haven't gone through." I looked at Yangi. "You didn't believe me?"

He shrugged.

"Can I see them?" I asked.

All three tensed as Happy slowly handed them over. The slips were all there. All I had to do was rip them in half. What could they really do? Half the restaurant was staring at us, including the security guards. They wouldn't dare touch me. But...I hesitated. The past hour of lying, and then lying about lying, only to lie once again, had left me giddy. I felt like a compulsive gambler; my goal was no longer to win my money back but to prove that I was the best bullshit artist at the table.

"Here." I handed the slips back to Happy. "If you think it's safe, use them. Uh, I've got to go to the bathroom."

Happy and Yangi were hissing like two teakettles when I returned, Yangi going yes, yes, yes, Happy nodding no, no, no. Their "friend," as befitted a thug whose sole duty was to break my legs, had no opinion.

"We have something else we want to show you," said Yangi as I sat down. He pulled out the credit card slips and tore them in half.

Happy put his head in his hands and moaned.

The new and improved plan was as follows: They would make forgeries of the original paintings (the original forged paintings, that is) and give these to the corporation backing the scheme, along with a note from me saying I was returning their paintings. I would then sell the original forged "antiques" in Paris as best I could. The three of us would split the profits. They figured I could sell the paintings for about ten thousand dollars.

The only catch was that it would cost about eight hundred

dollars to get the new forgeries made. They could raise four hundred but wanted me to put in the rest.

I pretended to go along, all the while planning to get on the next plane out of India. But I eventually gave them the cash. After all, if they'd conned me, I'd conned them. So in that sense, we were even. Moreover, if they weren't scamming me, I'd done a terrible thing, and four hundred dollars was a small price to pay to ensure I did not rob innocent people of what was in Indian terms a small fortune. And I still felt a connection with Yangi. I was sure it was he who had convinced Happy to destroy the credit slips. Before I left, I asked him one last favor.

"If all this was a scam, and I don't need to hurry to Paris to pick up the paintings, mail me this postcard," I said. I handed him a stamped postcard addressed to myself, care of the central post office in Sana'a, Yemen. "I will be out of the country and can make no problems for you by then."

the Man in the Red Hat

Coffee should be black as Hell,
strong as death and sweet as love.
Turkish Proverb

That was the postcard I received in Sana'a two months later. Yangi had written to let me know that our "business" was still on. I would have to abandon the idea of traveling to Turkey via the old spice routes and fly instead.

Still, despite all the eminently valid reasons I had for not going overland, I was besieged by feelings of guilt as I winged my way over the Arabian peninsula. My premise had been to travel using the same means coffee had taken four to ten centuries earlier. This was clearly a deviation. To compensate, I tried to imagine myself trudging through the desert far below, suffering the same heat and thirst as had the early coffee caravans. (*Stewardess? Could I have some more ice in my Coke, please?*) I kept an eye peeled for trilitys, the ancient stone markers that still delineate the caravan routes from Yemen to Mecca. I even tried to imagine that the wretched airline coffee was authentic Bedouin *qahwa* and the stewardess a Nubian coffee slave.

But it just wasn't the same.

MY PLANE LANDED IN THE TURKISH PORT OF IZMIR DURING ONE of the worst rainstorms in decades. I immediately took the next train to the village of Konya. When I got off the train twenty-four hours later, I climbed on the first bus I encountered and headed into town. It was hard to see what was going on outside on account of the rain, but after about twenty minutes I had the sense that we might be in the center and decided to get off. Since I couldn't communicate, I simply offered my open wallet to the driver's assistant, who, after an odd look, helped himself to the fare. Then he jumped out of the bus, grabbed my shoulder, and gave me a gentle shove.

A freezing rain was falling. Everything was covered in mud. But no one bothered me. The politeness of the Turks I'd met so far had been astounding. I'd come expecting sodomy and *Midnight Express*, and instead I got Miss Manners. Why, the entire airplane had burst into applause when our pilot had managed a successful landing in Izmir. The only sour note had been a fellow passenger who told me that hotels in Konya were so scarce, I'd probably have to sleep in the local jail.

"My friend," said a voice in English. "Where are you going?"

A teenage boy in a leather jacket was blocking my way. I told him I was lost. He took me to a rambling old building that reeked of urine. Another man showed me a room with a wood burning stove. One million lira, he said. One million? I thought sleepily. Then I realized it was five U.S. dollars. Beats prison, I thought, lying down on the rough woolen blanket. I was asleep instantly.

THE FRENCH, THE DUTCH, AND THE ETHIOPIANS EACH STYLE themselves as the heavy in making coffee the world's most popular drug. But it's the Turks who are The Man. They were the ones who'd controlled the port of Mocha during its heyday. A Turkish ambassador introduced the French to coffee. Retreating Turkish soldiers abandoned those fateful bags of beans at the gates of Vienna, and Turkish merchants addicted all of the Adriatic Coast.

My reason for coming to Konya, however, was our old friends the Sufi mystics. If it was the Sufis of Yemen who discovered coffee, it was the Turkish Sufis who spread it throughout North Africa and the Middle East. Konya was the headquarters for their most famous Sufi brotherhood, the Mevlanas, known as the whirling dervishes, because they achieve a religious ecstasy by first sharing a pot of ceremonial coffee and then spinning in one spot for hours on end. The week I arrived in Konya they were holding their greatest festival, the Wedding Night, celebrating their founder's death seven hundred years earlier.

I woke up from my nap completely disoriented. All I remembered about my trip was the plateau around Konya, an ocean of green that had swelled in one seamless wave up into the grey dawn. I had no memory of getting off the train or checking into the hotel. I noticed a business card lying on the bed.

Excellent! Quality! Priceliness!

Ataturk Shopping Center

Turkish Carpets

I remembered: The boy who'd brought me here had given it to me. He had a carpet shop. I decided to go get lunch.

"My friend!" The boy was waiting for me outside. "How was your nap?"

I scowled. How had he known I was sleeping?

"My name is Ahmed. You will come to my shop and take tea? Very close."

"Yes, hmm..." I said. "You have a carpet shop, yes?"

"Yes—but no sale! Money is not everything."

"We are of one mind." I put my hand on his shoulder to steady him for the bad news. "For you must realize that I have no interest whatsoever in purchasing a carpet."

"Of course!" He tried to pull away. "No problem!"

I tightened my grip. "No, no. I will gladly come for a chat. I will even drink your tea. I will not buy a carpet."

"Yes, yes..."

"Or a kil'm or a prayer rug..."

"No..."

"Or a shawl."

"No shawls!"

"So I have told you and you understand?"

"Yesyesyes! No buy shawls. Come!"

I ended up taking tea with a gloomy middle-aged man who owned the shop. We talked about business (terrible!), then the weather (awful!). He seemed a touch morose, so I cheered him up by telling him about New York. Everybody carries guns, I said. They're all high on drugs. It's common for people to swing in through the window and rob you while you eat dinner.

He shook his head in disgust. "But tourists, they still come?"

"I wouldn't recommend it," I said. "It's really much too dangerous. And the prices!"

A boy came in with a tray of tea.

"For example," he said. "A cup of tea would cost..."

"Three hundred thousand lira," I said. That's $1.25. "But why do you drink tea? I thought that Turks drank only coffee."

"No, maybe in the past. Now tea. It is our culture." He shook his head dolefully. "Turkey is a modern country now."

"It happens. But you know, I was told that in the old days, when the Ottomans ruled, a woman could get a divorce from her husband if he failed to provide her with enough coffee beans for her needs. Have you ever heard of this?"

"Beans?"

"Yes, you know." I made a shape with my hand. "They are—"

"Yes, yes, I know beans." He looked disgusted. "That is the most ridiculous thing I have ever heard."

And with that, he turned to his friend and ignored me. He didn't even look up when I left. I asked Ahmed, who was loafing around outside the shop, why his boss might be so offended by my question about the beans.

"Beans?" he shrugged. "Who knows? My friend, listen. There is a French girl in your hotel."

"Really?"

"Yes—I am telling you! You will help me catch her, yes?" He put his arm around my shoulder. "You catch her and bring her here to the carpet shop for me? We catch her together!"

"I'll let her know that you're looking for her," I said truthfully. "Now about the dervishes..."

"For tickets you must go to the istadyum."

"Istadyum?" I repeated. "What's that?"

"Istaydum!" he repeated, making a motion with both hands like someone shooting a basket. "Istadyum! Ees biscuit ball."

The whirling dervishes held their prayer ceremonies in a basketball stadium? At first I thought this was some special "tourist" performance, but it turned out that this was the only venue in which the government would allow the ceremony to take place. The whirling dervishes were actually illegal and had been so since the Ottoman Empire was overthrown in the early 1900s by the father of the modern Turkish republic, Mustafa Kemal Ataturk. One of the first things that Ataturk did when he came to power was root out everything associated with the Ottomans. He rewrote the Turkish language, he outlawed beards, he even changed the weekend from Islamic Friday to Sunday. The whirling dervishes were closely associated with the Ottomans, so he banned them outright, restricting the performance of their prayer ritual to once a year in Konya and then only as a "folk dance."

Knowing this made sense of a peculiar incident I later saw at the so-called Whirling Dervish Museum. It began when an older woman in a black veil knelt in the museum doorway and began chanting. Two guards instantly pulled her to her feet. After a heated discussion, they let her go into the museum. I noticed one plainclothes guard following her around, tugging at her veil and hissing. Finally she slapped something into his hand, and they parted. But I'd caught the flash of Turkish lira—baksheesh.

I noticed a number of people discreetly praying before an exhibit of an elaborately decorated cask with a four-foot-tall turban set at one end. It turned out that this was the turban that had belonged to the cult's founder, Mevlana Celealeddin-i Rumi, known in the West as the poet Rumi. The turban and the cask, which contained his body, were thought to possess magical powers. The supposed museum was actually a mosque, one of the holiest spots in Turkey, despite which any Muslim wishing to pray was obliged to pay off guards, who were under orders to prevent any kind of religious activity on the premises.

It's still a touchy issue, especially with the growing power of the Turkish Islamic right wing. When I went to that evening's "folk dance performance," the program book said only that, upon overthrowing the Ottomans, Ataturk visited Rumi's tomb and declared that "the large number of artifacts...in the convent and tomb rendered them a valuable museum collection." There was no mention of the cult being banned or of the resulting tension. Everyone going in to see the performance, however, was frisked for weapons.

I have no idea whether American basketball is actually popular in Turkey, but the place for that night's performance was the real thing, right down to the huge Coca-Cola banners hanging from the ceiling. The only difference was the twelve-piece orchestra wearing fezzes sitting under the northern hoop. The place was full, and no sooner had I sat down than the main lights went off. There was a wandering flute solo. A pink spotlight hit a man in a business suit who proceeded to sing one of the longest, slowest songs I've ever heard, both profoundly passionate and, to my ears, slightly cheesy. It all made me think of a Las Vegas lounge act, the way he gestured, his suit, the cordless microphone. Then I realized that I was probably watching a mutation of the Sufis' traditional coffee-sharing ceremony. His song had once been "the cries of devotion" that the dervishes sang out as they took coffee from the hand of their *sheykah* priest and achieved the *marqaha*, or coffee ecstasy, that was necessary for the night-long ceremonies. There are any number of descriptions of the ceremony from the eighteenth century, all roughly equivalent to the following excerpt from H. C. Lukas's *The City of the Dervishes*:

> *In the lower order of the dervishes they would share a red pot of coffee, taking the cup directly from the* sheykah's *hand, squatting in a circle, crying out thanks to God, "Help us, oh Allah!" and starting to sway. "Ya Meded, Ya Allah! Ya Meded!" As they get worked up the cry and the swaying becomes more intense, the cry changed to*

…llah, la ilaha illa, llah! There is no God but God!" *…to "Ya hu!" (Oh God!) The groups like the Howling Dervishes* [called Naqshibendi] *chant themselves into ecstasy. Some use the sword* [called Rufa'i].

The importance early Sufis attached to coffee is indicated not only by its use at the beginning of their prayer ceremony and their passing the cup from hand to hand (a ritual of intoxication in Islamic eyes). The clue to coffee's deeper significance is the color of the serving vessel. Almost all early manuscripts agree that the brew was served by the *sheykah* from a ceremonial red vessel. The color red had a special meaning to the dervishes. It symbolized the mystical union with God that was their goal in prayer and articles of that color were believed to stand on "the Threshold of the Spiritual World." In the ceremony I was about to see, the *sheykah* sits on a red pelt and so becomes, by virtue of the pelt's color, the living manifestation of Rumi. That the brew was handed out by the *sheykah* himself from a ritual red vessel suggests it was viewed as a sacred inebriant crucial in preparing the devotee for union with the Ultimate Reality (some Sufi groups still use hashish for this purpose).

As the forty-five-minute prayer song ended, twelve men wearing black shawls and fez hats shuffled onto the court one step at a time. They were the dervishes. The man waiting at the northern free-throw line was their *sheykah*. As each dervish came face-to-face with the *sheykah*, everyone bowed—*sheykah* to dervish, dervish to *sheykah*, dervish to dervish—in time to the orchestra's wailing music. There was a pause. The dervishes dropped their black shawls to reveal spotless white vests and skirts. Again they started shuffling around the court. This time each dervish was kissed on the cheek when he reached the *sheykah*, at which he peeled off into the center of the court and began to spin. Soon the court was filled with serenely smiling men, their white skirts billowing out about them as they spun round and round and round and round without any apparent effort.

Every facet of the ceremony is symbolic. The dervishes' black shawls represent their graves, their white skirts their shrouds, and the fezzes, banned by Ataturk, represent their tombstones. The music of the *bey* reed flute that precedes the ceremony is the song of the reed yearning to rejoin the reed bed, symbolizing the human spirit's desire to return to the Ultimate.

After spinning for twenty minutes, the dervishes stopped, and the shuffling-bowing-kissing procession began all over. The entire sequence was repeated four times, with each spinning cycle, called a *Selam*, inducing a different level of enlightenment. By the final *Selam* the dervishes have become living incarnations of the stars spinning in the heavens, an homage to the Koran stanza, "Whatever is in the skies or on earth invokes God."

The ceremony is a form of prayer and not designed as spectator sport. Watching it, I went from fascination to boredom to hypnotic trance. Traditional Sema ceremonies continue until dawn. Some sects slash at each other with swords as they whirl to show the intensity of their trance. Others howl in ecstasy. Out of respect for the audience, however, the dervishes in tonight's ritual achieved Ultimate Truth after a mere three hours of spinning. As the ceremony ended, the dervishes put their robes back on and returned to earth. Finally the *sheykah*, a small, hook-nosed man who had remained silent all evening, spoke.

Dogu da bati da Allah'indir,

nereye donerseniz Allah'in yonu orasidir.

Dogrusu Allah her yeri kaplarve her seyi bilir.

It was from the Koran, Surah Baqara 2:115. All fifteen hundred "folk dance lovers" stood to chant it with him.

To God belongs the East and the West,

and wherever you turn is the face of God.

...acing, the All-Knowing.

...ONE HAD WARNED ME AGAINST TAKING THE OVERNIGHT train from Konya to Istanbul. They said it took twice as long as the bus (nonsense), that it was unsafe (rubbish) and so overheated that passengers' clothing caught fire (this is actually true). It was just a 1920 train full of funky-smelling chairs and lit nonstop by that ubiquitous Turkish fluorescence that makes everybody look like a corpse, which is pretty much how I felt by the time I disembarked in Istanbul. The next morning I had to take a ferry from the train station to reach the city proper. Hulking mosques surrounded by knife-like minarets guarded the approaching shore. To the right, through the falling snow, I glimpsed the towering ruins of Istanbul's ancient walls. To the left, I could see the palaces of the Ottoman Empire. It seemed a heavy, gloomy, place and as the boat glided through the black waters of the Bosporus, I slipped into an exhausted depression.

Coffee arrived here at the height of the Islamic Ottoman Empire, when a couple of Syrians named Hakm and Shams opened a coffeehouse, circa 1555. Cafés were already quite common in places like Iran, but Istanbul's coffeehouses were the first truly secular settings for the sacred brew. Gone was any pretense of working oneself into religious ecstasy; men lounged and smoked and sipped. Some cafés offered poetry readings; others had singing girls and puppet shows. But most were devoted to gossip. Even pro-coffee scholars, like Abd al-Qadir al-Jaziri (writing in 1558), complained that the Sufi coffee ceremonies had been replaced by joking and tall tales.

"Things reached such a point that the coffeehouses were filled by professors, hypocritical mystics (Sufis), and idlers who did not work...so that there was not a seat to be had," wrote sixteenth-century historian Ibrahim Pecevi. "For people said there could be no place for enjoyment and rest equal to these."

To heighten their patrons' pleasure, Istanbul's cafés offered "special" coffees containing *faz 'abbas*, a blend of seven drugs and spices that included pepper, opium, and saffron. Other treats included honey-hash balls and *sheera*, hash or marijuana mixed with tobacco, which could be smoked in water pipes—or mixed into coffee, creating an Islamic speedball, a "life-giving thing...which they [addicts] were willing to die for," according to famed Ottoman writer Katib Celebi.

The vice of choice, however, was sex. According to the seventeenth-century English traveler George Sandys, cafés doubled as brothels, with "many coffamen [keeping] beautiful boyes who serves as stales [prostitutes] to procure them customers." Ottoman moralists called them "dens of abominable practices...with youths earmarked for the gratification of one's lusts." To enhance their experience, wealthy Turks sometimes perfumed their cups by holding them upside down over a brazier of smoldering myrrh, a technique traditionally used by Bedouin women to perfume their genitals before making love. Others laced up to thirty cups a day with the aphrodisiac *anbar*, which we know as ambergris. "The most general mode of doing this is to put about a carat weight of ambergris in a coffeepot and melt it over a fire; then make the coffee in another pot," wrote Edward Lane in his 1836 *Modern Egyptians*. "Others keep a piece in the bottom of a cup and pour in the coffee; a piece of the weight above will serve for two or three weeks."

Obviously this was something I wanted to investigate firsthand. However, a few visits to modern Turkish cafés convinced me that aphrodisiac coffee was a thing of the past. ("You want *love* coffee?") So I headed for Istanbul's spice bazaar, a former mosque on the banks of the Bosporus now crammed with parakeet food. Having come from the more primitive souks of

Yemen, Istanbul's bazaars made me feel as if the modern shopping mall was evolving before my eyes. It seemed to me the key difference lay in the sidewalk. The Yemenese street of rough paving stones oozing mud had been supplanted by Turkish pavements smooth as a baby's bottom. This completely changed the stall's needs. Yemenese stalls barricade themselves from the street's filth; Istanbul's merchants allow their goods to overflow. The additional space allows a greater variety of goods, in turn requiring a more complex display, hence individually packaged products. The merchants, too, are different. When you meet a Yemeni coffee man, you know him immediately. He smells delicious. His Turkish cousin stinks of cash.

He does, however, speak English.

"Yes, yes, of course I speak the English. *Sprechen Deutsch, parle français.*"

"*Habla español?*" I asked.

I asked because I had noticed that, while the merchants at Istanbul's Great Covered Bazaar advertised they spoke German, here at Misir Carisi, the spice bazaar, they all claimed to speak Spanish.

"It is bullshit," said the shopkeeper. "Competition! One puts up a sign saying he speaks Spanish, so all do the same."

I asked him if he had any ambergris.

He gave me a puzzled look and waved over a teenage boy who spoke better English.

"Bergris?" He'd never heard of it. "What is for?"

"Aphrodisiac," I said. "For love."

"Oh, love!" He pulled a bottle down from the shelf. The fluorescent pink label, shaped like a heart, featured a muscular man glistening with grease. "This is better," he said. "Ees Aphrodisiaque des Sultans."

"Not ambergris?" I asked. "I know people used to take it

with coffee..."

He shook his head disdainfully. "That old—this is scientific. Turkish people take this all the time. Have you seen Turkish family? Big! Not one, not two, but three, four ninas! Every day they take this, two spoons. This is big jar for family. You have family?"

"No." I pointed to the African figure with an enormous erection adorning the lid. "That's nice. And look, here, on the ingredients—it has amber."

"Oh, has many things," he said. "Seventeen ingredients. This is sultan's formula."

"Really?"

"That is why it is best. Sultan had biggest families. Three hundred wives!" He waved his hands excitedly. "You have seen Topkapi palace? The sultans had own factory there for making only the best and fresh, uh, how you say? Pills. Factory for men, factory for women."

I bought a bottle. "But you don't have the amber to put in coffee?"

"Amber in coffee?" He snapped his fingers. "You want not amber, you want *anbar* from the fish."

Of course. I had forgotten that *anbar* is Arabic for ambergris (neither has anything to do with amber), hence the confusion. Ambergris originates in sperm whales who have eaten too many giant deep-sea squids (the beaks irritate their tummies). This black, stinking secretion exposed to air, hardens into a resin-like material so fragrant that a single drop applied to paper remains fresh-smelling for forty years. It was generally found on deserted beaches, and was so desirable among the Turks that failure to hand it over to the sultan was punishable by death. Nobody, however, knew where it came from. The Chinese called it *lung sien hiang*, "dragon's spittle perfume," because they thought it came from drooling dragons sleeping by the edge of the sea.

To protect the whales it has now been banned, but the young man managed to acquire a piece about the size of half an M&M, dark and slightly sticky, which we sampled with coffee from a nearby stall. The smell had a truffle-like intensity: warm, rich, and leathery. I could definitely imagine why it would be thought a sexual enhancer.[1]

I again raised the question about the Ottoman custom of granting a woman divorce if her husband failed to provide her with adequate coffee beans—and got an interesting alternate explanation.

"My friend, he thinks the problem is translation," said the boy. "Beans—not enough beans!" He grabbed his testicles. "These are called beans. Not strong enough!" He patted the bottle of Sultan's Delight. "Must eat this."

The idea that coffee enhances your sexual prowess, with or without ambergris, is both right and wrong, for while coffee does not affect a man's or woman's performance, sperm exposed to caffeine swim faster and are much more likely to fertilize the woman's egg, thus making a man's "beans" potentially more potent. What's odd about the Ottomans' belief is that it was directly contradicted by the medical theories of the time. Under the Hippocratic theory of essential fluids and humors, coffee was thought to be a "dry" element that deprived the body of essential juices, particularly semen, "rendering men incapable of generation," according to scholar Simon Paulli. Coffee addicts were thought to literally pee themselves to death, "the body becoming a mere shadow of its former self, going into decline and eventually dwindling away," according to the tract *Istifa' al-safwa*. Doctors at the Medical University of Marseilles in the late 1600s

---

[1] Another coffee used as an aphrodisiac is the Peaberry coffee bean from Central America, called *caraiol*.

claimed that "ash" contained in coffee desiccated the entire body, particularly the central nervous system, which "dried up...producing general prostration and impotence."

The women of London found these scenarios of withered and flaccid manhood particularly alarming. By the 1670s their city was overrun with coffeehouses. When these medical reports became common knowledge, a group of females petitioned the mayor to ban the "hell-brew" coffee in order to preserve their sex lives. Their seven-page petition gives some compelling reasons. British gentlemen, it said, were the "ablest performers in Christendom...with lusty lads of eight hundred years fathering Sons and Daughters." These amazing feats of sexual prowess, however, came to an end when that "abominable, heathenish liquor called COFFEE...dried up their Radical Moisture...leaving them with nothing moist but their Snotty noses, and nothing stiff but their joints."

But a fuller extract is in order.

> *The Humble Petition and Address of Several Thousand of Buxome Good-Women, Languishing in Extremity of Want..."*
>
> *SHEWETH*
>
> *That since 'tis Reckon'd amongst the Glories of our native Country To be A paradise for women, it is too our unspeakable Grief we find of late that our gallants are become mere Cock-sparrows, fluttering things that come on with a world of Fury but in the very first Charge fall down Flat before us...all these qualities we can Attribute to nothing more than excessive use of the most pernicious Coffee, where Nature is Enfeebled and our men left with Ammunition Wanting; peradventure they Present but cannot give Fire....Certainly our Countrymen's palettes are become as Fanatical as their Brains. How else is it possible they should run a Whoreing to spend the money and time on a little base, black thick, nasty, Bitter, Stinking, Nauseous, Puddle-water (also known as Ninny's*

Broth and Turkish Gruel), so that those that have scarce twopence to buy their children bread must spend a penny each evening in this insipid stuff...

Wherefore we pray that drinking COFFEE be forbidden to all Persons under the Age of Threescore and that Lusty Nappy Beer and Cock Ale[2] be Recommended to General Use...so that our Husbands may (in time) give us some other Testimonies of the being Men, besides their Beards, and that they no more shall run the hazard of being Cuckol'd by Dildos.

In Hopes of A Glorious Reformation

London, 1674

[2] Cock Ale is made by adding a dead rooster to fermenting beer and is said to enhance sexual performance. A Scottish Highlands recipe from the 1500s goes like this: "Take ten gallons of ale and a large cock, the older the better; parboil the cock, flay him, and stamp him in a stone mortar until his bones are broken (you must gut him when you flay him). Then, put the cock into two quarts of sack, and put to it five pounds of raisins of the sun, some blades of mace, and a few cloves. Put all these into a canvas bag. Put the bag in the ale in a vessel. In a week or nine days bottle it up, fill the bottle just above the neck, and give it the same time to ripen as other ale."

War

At this time to refuse or to neglect to give coffee to their wives was a legitimate cause for divorce among the Turks.

William H. Ukers (1873–1945)

I NORMALLY DON'T USE GUIDES, but when Roger ("Call me Roger!") attached himself to me as I entered Istanbul's Topkapi palace, I was unable to resist. He was that perfect shade of geek that leaves you wondering, is he annoying? Is he amusing? Or is he just putting you on? A small man with a huge beak of a nose and a bleat like a rubber ducky makes when you squeeze it.

According to Roger, the Topkapi palace was home to the Ottoman sultan. It had all the modern conveniences—heated floors, indoor and outdoor swimming pools, a riverfront view, and, of course, castrated doormen. It contained fifteen separate kitchens, now transformed into a museum of culinary history that gives an excellent overview of how coffee's acceptance by the Islamic elite led to the creation of the modern coffee cup. Originally Turks had sipped their *qahwa* from the same kind of vessel used by the Ethiopians, a handleless bowl the size of an egg. For the sultan someone created a bowl holder, rather like an eggcup, called a *zarf*. There are a number of fine examples at Topkapi's culinary museum, gold and diamond encrusted, serviceable in a quotidian way. Over time the Turks added little handles to the side of the *zarfs*. Finally some Einstein moved the handle from the *zarf* to the cup, dumped the *zarf*, and boom! The modern demitasse was born.

The Turkish technique for brewing coffee echoes the Ethiopian coffee ceremony, in which a single pot is brewed and served three times for friendship. Turks boil ground coffee, water, and sugar three times in rapid succession and pour it, grounds and all, into a demitasse. If there are guests, it is important that they get plenty of the *wesh*, or *crema*, that crowns a properly done espresso.[1] Afterward, the host is supposed to pour the grounds out onto the saucer and read the guests' futures. The sultan, Portal of Eternal Light to his friends, had a slightly more elaborate coffee ceremony involving up to thirty people, including a First Minister of the Coffee, according to *Souvenir sur le harem imperial* by Leila Hanoum:

> *It arrives already prepared in a golden coffee pot* (ibrik) *which rests on coals contained in a golden basin hung from three chains which are gathered at the top and held by a slave... Two other girls hold*

[1] The tea equivalent to *crema* is "Cream of the Fragrant Dust," a light froth created when powdered tea is beaten vigorously.

golden trays with little coffee cups made of fine Savoy or Chinese porcelain…The First Minister of the Coffee takes a zarf from the tray, places a cup in it and then, with a small piece of quilted linen that is always on the tray, she pours the coffee…Next, with her fingertips she grasps the base of the zarf, which rests on the end of her index finger supported by the tip of her thumb, and offers it to the Sultan with a gesture of infinite grace and dexterity.

Roger thought all this quite dull.

"Here is most important!" he said, shoving me through a crowd of Malaysian Muslims wearing white jogging suits and gathered about what looked like a piece of old rug. "This is Mohammed's beard."

No disrespect to the Prophet's Whiskers (May They Grow Ever Longer!), but I was more interested in the Sultan's Harem, a two-hundred room complex, which supposedly no man other than the sultan had ever entered. I discovered that this was not exactly true.

"Here is where the Black Eunuchs slept," droned Roger as we entered a series of rooms at the harem's entrance. "Outside were the White Eunuchs. Only the Black Eunuchs were allowed inside.

"Yes!" he continued, before I could ask. "And there was a very good reason for this. This is because sometimes the operation was not always a success."

"I'm sorry, Roger," I said. "What operation would that be?"

"The removal of the thing." He blinked. "The manly organ. Sometimes, if the operation was not a success, the eunuch could perhaps get a woman with baby."

"You mean they missed?" I asked.

"Perhaps. And that is why only the Black Eunuchs were allowed within the harem. It was thought possible to see in the baby's face if the father was a black man of Africa and not the sultan."

I was impressed. "I'd never have thought of that," I said.

Roger gave me a dry look. And that, my friend, it said, is why the sultan was the sultan and you are just a tourist.

The harem was a lively place. Wives poisoned each others' children, sons had their mothers strangled, and brothers had other brothers' eyes put out. One of its more exclusive features was the Cage, four inner rooms where the sultan's brothers were imprisoned from birth until death. Meant to prevent wars of succession, it was considered a humanitarian alternative to the tradition of having the sultan murder his own siblings upon ascending to the throne.

The nastiest of the sultans was coffee-hating Murad IV. Born in 1612, he became sultan at the age of eleven and had ordered the strangulation of five hundred soldiers by the time he was twenty. He then dispatched two of his brothers, only sparing the third because his mother convinced him that the remaining bro' was too loony to ever take the throne. Murad quickly earned the nickname "Hasty" for executing a group of ladies who had sung in public (disturbing the peace). It is said he particularly enjoyed beheading men with fat necks.

He often wandered the city in disguise, searching for traitors. One night in 1633 he and (perhaps) his vizier dressed themselves as commoners and crept out into the darkened city. Being an alcoholic, the sultan made his first stop at a tavern which, according to eighteenth-century English traveler John Ellis, he found full of "people getting drunk and singing songs of love." His next stop was one of Istanbul's many cafés, where Ellis reports he "observed several sensible and grave persons soberly discoursing on the affairs of the empire, blaming the administration" for a variety of problems. Murad listened for a while and then crept back to the palace.

Soon after this Murad banned coffee. Istanbul's cafés were razed. People caught drinking were beaten. If again apprehended, they were sewn into a leather bag and tossed into the Bosporus to drown. Ships carrying coffee were sunk. Murad claimed coffeehouses were a fire hazard, but his real concern was that they encouraged insubordination by providing his subjects with a meeting place that invited sober discussion. His anticoffee campaign was the first purely secular coffee suppression, as opposed to the earlier religious ones, and perhaps the first politically motivated campaign against a mind-altering substance. But he also had a personal hatred for the water pipe which invariably accompanied a Turkish cup of coffee. According to foreign visitors, Murad started roaming the streets with his executioner, instantly beheading anyone he found drinking coffee or smoking.[2]

"Where the Sultan went on his travels...his halting places were always distinguished by a terrible rise in executions," wrote contemporary Nicolo di'Conti. "Even on the battlefield he was fond of surprising men in the act of smoking [or drinking coffee], whom he would punish by beheading or crushing their hands and feet." Others reported that he liked to humiliate smokers by forcing a pipe through their noses and making them ride about Istanbul before personally beheading them.

Although it seems incredible, from ten thousand to one hundred thousand people were executed for these crimes. Thousands more were mutilated. Islamic historians of the time reported that for decades Istanbul remained as "desolate of cafés as the heart of the ignorant." Taverns, although also banned, were allowed to stay open.

After Murad died, from alcohol poisoning, Istanbul's

[2] Murad was given a facetious honor by the seventeenth-century English coffeehouse Ye Great Coffee House, which issued coffee tokens bearing a picture of his head and the inscription "Morat ye Great Men did mee call/Where Eare I came I conquer'd all." These coffee tokens were one of the first examples of private currency and were accepted as cash in the immediate neighborhood until the government banned them outright.

coffeehouses gradually began to reappear. Nonetheless, the damage was done. Dispossessed coffee vendors had gone abroad to seek their fortune and within a decade began to pop up in Italy, France, and Austria

Murad's suppressions did have the effect of helping to restore order in the empire. The Ottomans consolidated their hold over their eastern territories and then turned their attention to Romania and Bulgaria. Within thirty years of Murad's death they controlled all of Eastern Europe, and in 1683 they marched on Vienna, home to the Hapsburg Empire, then the largest political entity in the West. Their first act, upon arriving at the gates of Vienna, was to shoot over the city's walls a pillowcase with a demand of surrender inside.

> *To You, Generals, Governors, and Noble Citizens of Vienna, we make known by these presents, according to the Orders we have received from the most Serene, Most Mighty, most Redoubted, and Mightiest Emperor of the Universe, our Master, the true Image of God upon Earth, who, by the Grace of the Most High, in imitation of our holy Prophet Mahomet Mustapha, to whom be Honor, Glory, and Benediction, hath rendered Himself by the multitude of His Miracles the greatest of all Sovereigns of the one and the other World, and most August of Emperors, who, having caused our innumerable Armies, protected always by Divine Providence, to come hither, We are resolved to take Vienna.*

Please surrender, is what they were saying. The Viennese declined. The Turks, all three-hundred thousand of them, pitched tents—about twenty-five thousand of them—and settled in for the summer.

I LEFT ISTANBUL AND HEADED FOR VIENNA TWO DAYS AFTER MY tour of the Topkapi palace. It was December 23. As we snaked our way out of the city, I kept pressing my face against the window to see what could be seen through the falling snowflakes. I went to sleep while it was still light out. By morning the snowfall had lightened, and I could see the countryside. Leafless trees, dull wet earth. There was virgin snow everywhere, glittering during the day, turning luminous blue at dusk. After a year in the tropics, the sight made me want to weep with joy.

The only problem was that my ticket had the wrong date on it. Turkish conductors waved me on with an exasperated "*Bismallah!*" The Bulgarians wanted to arrest me as a spy but settled for a bribe. The Romanian conductor seemed content to nag me to death, returning every half hour and demanding to see my ticket yet again, muttering, "Ees no goo, ees no goo!" Clearly he wanted a bribe of his own. But one payoff per day is my policy.

My Romanian cabinmate told me not to worry. "Berry Romany," he said of the conductor. "Ees jes de talk." I loved my cabinmate. He looked just like Roman Polanski. His shoes smelled worse than mine. Best of all, he spoke no English. I too liked the conductor—the way his chins shook in bureaucratic outrage, and his teeny blue conductor's cap. And Polanski was right. By the time we reached the other side of the Transylvania Mountains, Christmas morning, we were all three sitting in the cabin sharing my Turkish tangerines. The conductor whipped up some fiercely black java, syrupy and delicious, which we drank out of heavy porcelain cups decorated with a dashing red Romanian Rail Systems logo. It was nice to be back in Europe.

I'd taken the Transylvanian route to Vienna in order to put as much distance as possible between myself and the Serbian conflict. *Plus ça change, plus ça reste la même*, a French saying all too distressingly true of the current situation. Today it's Christians raping and killing Muslims; under the Ottoman rule, it had been Muslims playing the heavy. The Ottomans had used this area as a recruiting ground for military slaves. Men were carried off, women were forced into harems, and children were left behind to starve. In many respects it was identical to Serbia's ethnic cleansing atrocities.

But I saw none of this. I arrived in Vienna late on December 25. The train station at Westbanhopf was deserted. I wandered for an hour among the city's grand old buildings, so clean and well kept, so sterile and empty—so *different* from Turkey or Yemen or India. Everything was a hundred years old but looked like it had been built yesterday. The streets were immaculate. Empty streetcars rolled by. But no people. You would have thought the city had been abandoned.

THAT WAS PRETTY MUCH THE SITUATION BY THE SECOND MONTH of the Ottoman siege. Everybody who could, including King Leopold, had fled. Vienna's population had dwindled to seventeen thousand. There was nothing to eat. Plague broke out. Meanwhile, the Ottoman Turks were digging a series of secret tunnels and planting explosives under the city walls.

What the Turkish leaders did not know was that an army of about fifty thousand mainly Polish soldiers was approaching the city. They also were unaware that the Viennese knew all about the tunnels, thanks in part to a spy named Franz Kolschitzky. Kolschitzky had lived in Istanbul and could pass for a Turkish soldier. After the Viennese learned when the Turks planned to blow up the walls, he managed to get through the Turkish lines and inform the Polish generals.

On September 8, the Turks blew up their tunnels, breaching Vienna's walls in four separate spots. In poured the Turks. The Viennese held out until evening, when, during a final attack by the Turkish elite troops, the Poles set off a huge fireworks display from a nearby hill and attacked. The fact that they were outnumbered six to one did not matter as much as it might have, because the sultan had focused all his resources on the city, leaving his rear unguarded. The Poles rushed in and spread havoc. Night fell. When they woke up, considerably worried that once the surprise was over, they'd get massacred, the Poles found the Turks had fled. Three hundred years of Islamic expansionism had come to a screeching halt.

It was a historical turning point, although not for the obvious reason. Among the twenty-five thousand camels the Turks had left behind, the Viennese found dozens of bags of mysterious green beans. Everyone thought they were camel food. But the spy Kolschitzky recognized them as coffee beans and, when asked to name his reward for his role in saving the city, he asked for nothing more than said bags of coffee, with which he intended to open Vienna's first coffeehouse. Later he decided the city should also give him a building in which to house his café. Later still, he requested some start-up money. Some indentured servants to work as waiters? The keys to the queen's chastity belt?

"KOLSCHITZKY WAS A SPY AND A FRAUD, A MISER AND A CHEAT—so some say." Herr Diglas brightened up. "But a good story is always worth something."

The Viennese take their food history seriously, and Kolschitzky's role in the creation of the city's café society had recently been the subject of considerable debate. The accepted version had always been that Kolschitzky used the abandoned coffee beans to open Vienna's first café, the Blue Bottle. However, some historians—including Herr Diglas, a pear-shaped café proprietor who heads the Viennese Coffeehouse Association—contend that there were actually half a dozen spies involved and that the first official coffeehouse was opened by a spook named Johnannes Diodato.

Whatever. The important thing is not who opened the first Viennese coffeehouse but what they did there, for it was in these cafés that the Turkish habit of leaving grounds in one's coffee ended. The events surrounding this milestone are lost in the mists of time. We can only speculate that it was in response to those oh-so-fastidious Viennese finding UFOs—Unidentified Floating Objects—in their morning cup.

According to Diglas, Vienna is also where adding milk or cream in coffee first became common. This, however, is conjecture. All we know is that it was a European innovation, because the Turks (like the Hindus) believed that combining milk with coffee caused leprosy. We also know that early London coffee society did not generally use milk. This leaves the Italians or the Viennese as the most likely innovators, since both were among the earliest coffee drinkers in continental Europe.[3] Diglas pointed out that the two countries have milk-based brews, both completely different but bearing similar names—cappuccino from Italy, and Vienna's *kapuziner*.

"The elderly ladies, some still know of this drink, *da kapuziner*," Diglas said. "They come in and ask for one and they know exactly what they want—just the right shade of brown, like a monk's robe." He shrugged. "Ahhh, but I think of all my waiters only one knows what that drink is now. Too young, it goes, it is forgotten..."

He called over an elderly waiter and asked him if he knew how to make a *kapuziner*. Negative. Nobody in Diglas's café, a classically Viennese establishment full of people drinking coffee and gorging on sumptuous cakes, knew how to make the

[3] There is a 1625 etching from Cairo showing what appears to be milk and coffee combined. The practice, however, was almost nonexistent.

drink. Bear in mind, these waiters are men in their fifties and sixties who know how to brew Vienna's over twenty types of coffee drinks.

"Besides, there is no recipe, you know," Diglas said. "It is just the color. You must know the exact shade of the monk's robe, and the amount of milk will vary according to the strength of the bean."

The monks Diglas mentioned are from the Capuchin order of the Catholic Church, the namesake for both *kapuziner* and cappuccino. The story of how the order became associated with the drink begins in the Italian village of Assisi. It was here, around 1201, that a fellow named Giovanni began to act a little odd. He wandered about naked. He talked to birds. If it had happened today, he would have been institutionalized. But it was the medieval period, so he was canonized. We know him today as St. Francis of Assisi.

A religious order immediately sprang up around his teachings and just as quickly splintered into a dozen factions that spent their time pooh-poohing each other. Then came little Matteo da Bascio. He was a quiet Franciscan monk who loved St. Francis and his poverty and his birds and his simplicity. One day the ghost of St. Francis visited him to complain about his order's decadent behavior. What grabbed Matteo's attention, however, was the saint's outfit—he was wearing a pointed hood, not the square one mandated by the order. Outraged, Matteo petitioned the Vatican for the right to wear a peaked hood. The pope acquiesced. The other Franciscans, however, were furious with his new holier-than-thou habit and threw Matteo into a dungeon. Matteo refused to give up his new hat. The Franciscans, in turn, refused to let him go. It grew so ridiculous that the pope intervened and created a completely new order just for Matteo, thus liberating him from Franciscan authority.

And so was born the Capuchin order, *cap* meaning hat or hood in Italian, a reference to the pointed hood Matteo was fond of and, later, to the "cap" of whipped cream or steamed milk (perhaps we should call it a halo?) that crowns the cappuccino. Vienna's *kapuziner*, however, has no cap and was supposedly created when a local member of this fashion-conscious order added milk to his coffee so it would match his dark brown robe. When I made inquiries about this at Vienna's Capuchin monastery, I was rudely told to go away.

"We are not a coffee chain. Do you understand?" sputtered an agitated monk. "We are a religious order! "

The Capuchins are irked by the whole business because they think the cappuccino's head of whipped cream (or steamed milk) insults their order by implying that a Capuchin monk is an airhead.

"A cappuccino is no joking matter here in Vienna," Diglas explained when I told him about the monk's reaction. "We take our coffee very, very seriously.."

My friend the Countess, whom I met the next day, agreed.

"YOU SEE, HOW YOU TAKE A THING EES AS IMPORTANT AS vat you take—Americans tink to dreenk der cappucheeno like a Coca-Cola. No!" The Countess flicked her spoon contemptuously at my cup. Lumps of dirty whipped cream drifted about a gray sea of espresso. Shards of melted chocolate oozed over the cup's lip. "Dis ees de drink of de royal Hapsburg family. And look vat you have done!"

I met the Countess, my nickname for her, in Café Demel, a place that prides itself on serving cappuccino exactly as at the turn of the century: strong brewed coffee, not espresso, a bowl of chocolate shavings, and a dome of *schlagober* (whipped cream) on a silver platter. The Countess had been so horrified by my attempt to consume this concoction that she volunteered to give me a lesson.

"You Americans have been spoiled by zee straw," she said. The Countess looked a bit like Vienna herself, old but beautiful, or at least well maintained. Certainly rich. But cruel, especially about the mouth, the lips of which were lacquered to a Porsche-like gloss. Pearls gleamed milky white among the family of small animals draped about her neck.

One of Café Demel's black-clad waitresses placed a fresh cappuccino on our table, and the Countess proceeded with my lesson. First, she piled her *schlagober* on the coffee, sprinkling it lightly with the chocolate shavings. "You eat zo." She made a delicate gesture with her spoon, then a vicious stabbing motion. "Not like zat. You are not killing somezing, ya?"

I'd stabbed down through the whipped cream in an attempt to blend the coffee with the cream. The proper way, according to the Countess, was to let the whipped cream melt into the coffee while you nibbled it and the chocolate shavings. When the whipped cream receded to within a half inch of the coffee, it was permissible to break the crust. You could raise the cup to your lip at this juncture. Under no circumstances, however, would you drink or allow your lips to touch the whipped cream. Instead, you inhale the elixir, sucking the coffee toward you through the *schlagober* and spraying a java-flavored patina upon your palate. A slight slurping sound is permissible.

"Zen, ven all is safe and zee *schlagober* is gone, you may drink. Zee coffee in zee cup should be like zis shade of brown, you see?

"Zee first part, ven you eat zee *schlagober* of the cappuccino, is like childhood, Steuart—all sveet, light, and frivolous. Zee second part is like middle age." The Countess paused. "But I have nozing poetic to say about zat."

She went on, "And za last is old age, black and bitter, perhaps, but maybe zee best part for zose who have developed a taste."

ON MY LAST DAY IN VIENNA, DURING A VISIT TO THE MUNICIPAL museum, I stumbled across a portrait of the vizier who led the campaign against the city in 1683. In the painting, Kara Mustafa looks a chubby-faced fellow. Anxious. Hardly the face of a tyrant. Then again, if the painting was done as he marched back to Istanbul, Kara had had every right to look meek. The sultan gave him a dog's welcome when they met. In fact, he had Kara strangled in front of his own family and his head stuffed.

The synergistic bond between the decline of the Ottomans and the spread of coffee did not end at the seige of Vienna. In 1670, ten years before the siege, the ingredients for every cup of coffee in the world originated from within the Ottoman Empire. The beans came from Yemen, sugar from Africa. In 1671, French minister Jean Baptiste Colbert built a sugar mill in Marseilles. Coffee, stolen from the Turks a hundred years earlier, began to flourish in the New World. By 1730, even the Turks were making their coffee with products grown in Christian-controlled territories.

Next to the vizier's portrait in the museum hung an old Ottoman flag, a field of white emblazoned with a red crescent moon. Curiously, their flag's crescent also became a dish representing their decline.

Back in 1683, during the Turkish siege of Vienna, a baker named Peter Wender heard a curious tick! tick! while working late at night in his basement bakery. It was the Turks digging their secret tunnels. He warned the city officials and later created a bread roll shaped like the Turks' crescent moon to advertise his contribution to the war effort. Using bread as political propaganda was quite common back then; when King Gustav Adolf II of Sweden ravaged Germany only fifty years earlier, every gingerbread in the area was soon decorated with Adolf's face transformed into a child-eating monster.

After the Turks were defeated, it became the Viennese custom to serve Wender's little crescent roll, called the *pfizer*, with morning coffee. And there it would have ended except that a century later a seventeen-year-old Viennese princess named Marie Antoinette moved to Paris to marry Louis XVI, king of France. Homesick, she insisted that the French bakers learn to make *pfizer* for her breakfast. The bakers added butter and yeast, and since it would have been unthinkable for a queen of France to eat anything but "French" pastry, they renamed it *le croissant*, which means crescent in French.

So was born the most politically loaded meal in the world—the Continental breakfast of coffee stolen from the Turks and pastry shaped to mock their flag. But when hundreds of millions of Europeans begin their day with the combo, they are doing more than unwittingly commemorating the Turkish defeat at Vienna. They are participating in a rite that lies at the heart of the most profound pharmacological revolution in European history.

the Revolution

In a coffee house just now among the rabble I
bluntly asked, which is the treason table.

Malone, 1618

BY THE TIME THE TURKS HAD abandoned those bags of beans at the gates of Vienna, coffee had made cameo appearances in the ports of Venice, London, France, and Holland. The first written reference to it being consumed by a European occurs in correspondence dated 1615, but it's unlikely that even the most intrepid gourmands were tippling it regularly before the middle of the century.

To appreciate the significance of this new recreational drug, however, you first have to appreciate what redneck backwater Europe was four hundred years ago. There were no books. Fewer movies. The music was *awful*. And the food...Pepper was unknown, salt rare, and sugar had just made a debut. Basically, it was a lot like Nebraska on a slow weekend—church or beer. Europeans, however, had the sense to combine the two. Paris in 1660 had over one hundred religious holidays and every one of them culminated in the marathon drinking competitions so popular then. "They must swallow half, then all of a drink in one gulp without stopping to take a single breath," wrote one German in 1599, "until they sink into a complete stupor...(then) the two heroes emerge and guzzle in competition with one another."

Drinking raised your social status, hence the phrase "drunk as a lord." Toasting was a way of displaying your wealth. He who drank the most was also rewarded with the piece of toasted bread floated in the glass (hence the name). The writer Fortunatus considered these toasting competitions tantamount to suicide, with participants "carrying on like madmen, each competing in drinking to the other's health...so that a man had to consider himself lucky to come away with his life." At night, Europe's cities were full of drunkards "weaving from side to side, stumbling and staggering, falling into the mud, their legs splayed out wide enough for a coach to pass through."

Beer was not only the main means of celebrating, it was second only to bread as a source of nourishment. Every housewife baked bread, every housewife brewed beer. "People subsist more on this drink than they do on food," wrote Placutomus in 1551.

Beer thickened with eggs and poured over bread was the original Continental breakfast and remained popular in Germany until the mid-1700s. Since hot beverages were rare and water unsafe, workers took midmorning beer breaks. Beer for breakfast, ale for lunch, stout with dinner, and a few mugs in between. The average Northern European, including women and children, drank *three liters of beer a day*. That's almost two six-packs, but often the beer had a much higher alcoholic content. People in positions of power, like police, drank much more. Finnish soldiers were given a ration of five liters of strong ale a day (as much alcohol as about seven six-packs, or about forty cans). Monks in Sussex made do with twelve cans' worth.

Almost everything had some liquor in it, especially medicines. Anything that wasn't deliberately fermented went off in the summer heat. In the winter, the beer froze, causing the alcohol to separate into high-proof liquor. We can be sure the resulting moonshine did not go to waste. To make matters worse, the main nonalcoholic source of nutrition, bread, is now believed to have been plagued with the hallucinogenic fungus ergot, the base ingredient for LSD. Drunk doctors, tipsy politicians, hungover generals: the plague, famine, and war. Add a pope on acid, and medieval Christianity starts to make a whole lot of sense.

So it's no surprise that booze was one of Martin Luther's first targets when he set about reforming the Catholic Church in the mid-1500s. Followers like the Capuchins printed posters of a drunken demon with a pig's head and bird's claws, the original "Demon Alcohol," and banned drinking contests. The only reaction was the formation of Europe's first temperance league, a group of Germans whose members limited themselves to a mere seven glasses of wine per meal. Otherwise, Europe staggered along as it always had. Doctors continued to advise patients to drink themselves unconscious at least "once a month...as it stimulates general well-being." One third of England's farmland was dedicated to growing barley for beer; one in seven buildings was a tavern.

Martin Luther's attempts to limit drinking failed because he had offered no alternative. Then came the great Ottoman coffee suppression of the 1640s and, within ten years, Europe's first coffeehouse opened in Oxford, England.[1] Cafés soon appeared in London, where, coincidentally, the Puritans had just seized control of Parliament.

When the sweet Poison of the Treacherous Grape
Had acted on the world a general rape;...
Coffee arrives, that grave and wholesome Liquor
That heals the stomach and makes the genius quicker.
Anonymous Puritan, 1674

THE TEETOALING PURITANS JUMPED ON THIS "BLACK WINE" AS A God-given alternative to beer. Better than an alternative, because it was thought to cure drunkenness. Sylvester DuFour's pamphlet *Traitez nouveau et curieux du café, du thé, et du chocolat* reported that coffee "sobers you up instantaneously, or in any event it sobers up those who are not fully intoxicated." Nonsense, of course, although recent tests indicate that the equivalent of two cups of coffee actually reverses some of alcohol's milder effects in a person with up to 0.04 percent alcohol blood levels (0.1% is considered intoxicated). This kind of mild alcoholic fog, however, was what most plagued Europe at the time, the "dizziness in the brain" that struck clerks after their midmorning beer break, according to private correspondence from the time. The growth of coffeehouses not only sobered up the clerks but slowly ended the midmorning pint altogether, according to historian James Howell. In 1652 there was exactly one coffeehouse in London. By 1700 there were over two thousand.

The confluence of the Puritans and coffee, however, did not

[1] The Oxford café was opened in 1650 by a Middle Eastern Jew. London's first was opened in 1652 by Pasqua Rosee, the namesake for the San Francisco chain Pasqua. His café is now a tavern called Jamaica Inn.

exist on the Continent. In the early 1600s Pope Clement VIII was even asked by his bishops to ban the "diabolical hell brew," apparently on the grounds that its black color and ritualistic use by the Sufis made it a Satanic perversion of the Eucharist wine. He declined—after trying a cup and liking it—but the Catholic heebie-jeebies helped ensure that continental Europeans kept breakfasting on beer-soup for almost one hundred years after their English competitors had made the switch.

Aside from sobering up the workplace, coffeehouses gave Brits an alternative to taverns in which to meet and talk. Taverns were not the safest place to discuss politics or religion. Everybody was armed or drunk, usually both, and proprietors sensibly discouraged heated discussions. Coffeehouses, on the other hand, encouraged political debate, which was precisely why King Charles II banned them in 1675 (he withdrew the ban in eleven days). Even worse, from the monarchists' point of view, cafés posted rules urging:

Gentry, tradesmen, sit down together,
Pre-eminence of place none here should mind
But take the next fit seat that he can find
Nor need any, if finer person come,
Rise up to assigne to them his room.

This democratic inclination manifested itself most forcefully in London's famous Turk's Head Coffeehouse, where the ballot box, the foundation of modern democracy, first appeared so customers could safely voice their opinions on controversial political topics. This innovation occurred after the repressions of Oliver the Great and ensured that the government spies who plagued the café could not identify "traitors."

There were, of course, some problems. Hot drinks were relatively rare at the time. DuFour had to advise his readers not to lap them up like a dog, "nor put your tongue in the cup."

People were confused over the spoon's role, using it either to "cool" this oddly hot brew by pouring it back and forth or to eat it like soup. They added mustard and champagne and mint and molasses and roasted carrots. (Amazingly, English coffee, as horrible as it was, was better than their first tea, the leaves of which the Brits ate as a boiled vegetable.)

Coffee, however, was more than a mere substitute for beer. It is a stimulant, both physical and mental, and its usurpation of a depressant like alcohol caused changes that echoed, to a word, the ancient prayer of the coffee-chewing cults of Ethiopia, which goes, you may recall, like this:

Coffeepot give us peace
coffeepot let children grow
let our wealth swell
please protect us from evils.

Coffee's ability to "swell our wealth" was manifested most noticeably in Britain, where coffeehouses became headquarters for some of the world's most powerful businesses, including Lloyd's of London (Lloyd's Coffeehouse) and the London Shipping Exchange (Baltic Coffeehouse) and East India Company (Jerusalem Café). The physical design of British coffeehouses also set the pace for the modern office. Tables set aside for certain groups of merchants turned into curtained stalls for greater privacy. These became offices or cubicles, which to this day remain gathered about a common pot. Until recently the messengers at the British Stock Exchange were called waiters, a holdover from the not too distant days when the exchange was an actual coffeehouse with waiters.

Other cafés evolved into centers for the arts and sciences. Isaac Newton hung out at the Grecian Coffeehouse; Will's Café was the haunt of writers like Jonathan Swift and Alexander Pope and painters like Hogarth frequented Old Slaughter's. As cafés became more specialized, keeping current by visiting became impractical. Then a man named Richard Steele decided to publish a weekly compilation of the most interesting gossip collected from the coffeehouses. To help keep the café's flavor, each section had a "correspondent's desk" at the appropriate establishment; poetry came from Will's Coffeehouse, foreign news from St. James Coffeehouse, arts and entertainment from White's. Steele also had his "reporters" write in dialogue to give the reader the illusion he was actually sitting in a café overhearing a real conversation. Up until then, the writing of lifelike dialogue had been viewed as being beneath an author's notice. "Until the time...writers had not practiced the studied simplicity of true conversation," writes English literary historian Harold Routh. "It was here [at the coffeehouse] that men learnt to unravel literary ideals in a style that was colloquial as well as cultured."

Intelligent people discussing interesting things in an intelligible manner. Quite a concept. Steele's newsletter became *Tatler*, the first modern magazine; his idea of correspondents and sections provided the prototype for the modern newspaper, the one institution that all agree is essential for a vital democracy (London's second oldest newspaper is *Lloyd's News*, which began as a bulletin board in Lloyd's Coffeehouse.) Small wonder that pamphleteers of the time wrote that "coffee and commonwealth came in together...to make a free and sober nation." Coffeehouses had made civilized conversation into a popular sport.

Measuring how recreational drugs alter societies is almost impossible. Analyzing how they affect the individual, however, is a little easier. If you drink three liters of ale, your ability to remember anything you were taught decreases by up to 80 percent. Conversely, coffee increases memory capacity. Drunk, you'd be more likely to resort to violence. More importantly, if pregnant women drank only one third the average three liters of ale a day—and since drinking was considered healthy, there's no reason to think they didn't—their newborns' IQ-level would have been diminished 7 percent. If they drank one liter above that average, almost half of their children would have been born retarded due to fetal alcohol syndrome.

Based on this kind of reasoning, one might conclude that the average medieval European was a thuggish idiot. That's silly. But try having a liter of strong ale with breakfast tomorrow (that's three bottles) and see how your day goes. We all know how it went when Europe changed from a culture addicted to depressants to one high on stimulants (at least during the day). Within two hundred years of Europe's first cup, famine and the plague were historical footnotes. Governments became more democratic, slavery vanished, and the standards of living and literacy went through the roof. War became less frequent and more horrible. For better or worse, the ancient Ethiopian coffee prayer had been answered with a vengeance.[2]

I STARTED THIS COFFEECENTRIC HISTORY OF HUMANITY IN JEST. After all, people have made similar charts based on the rise and fall of the hemline, and it would be absurd, even for me, to fail to acknowledge that historic events are spawned by a myriad of circumstances. But the coincidences at times seem overwhelming. When coffee was the sole provenance of the Arabs, their civilization flourished beyond all others. Once the Ottomans got hold of the bean, they became the most powerful and tolerant nation on the planet. Its early appearance in Great Britain helped jump-start that nation's drive for world dominance. It was in the cafés of Paris that the French Revolution was born.

---

[2] Interestingly, renowned cultural theorist Michel Foucault believes his famous "rationalization" of Western civilization started the same year that Europe's first café opened.

Napoleon, a coffee lover equal to any, then led his countrymen to the domination of Europe, only to fall almost immediately after foolishly banning Paris's beloved petit noir; he repented, and his dying request was for a cup of St. Helena's espresso. As colonists, the Americans actually made tea illegal. They replaced it with joe, causing an inevitable power shift that continues today, with Japan, traditionally tea-consuming, now doting on the finest Jamaican Blue Mountain.

Only three times has the West voluntarily dosed itself with mind-altering agents: alcohol starting at an unknown date, caffeine in the seventeenth century, and psychedelics in the late twentieth. How alcohol affected early society is impossible to measure, and the jury is still out on psychedelics. But it's worth noting that coffee (or caffeine) and psychedelics have been associated with strikingly similar cultural revolutions. Richard Steele drinking coffee and talking about reforming the monarchy is the same person as Abbie Hoffman smoking a joint and plotting how to resist the Vietnam War. Voltaire's caffeinated cynicism was as symptomatic of his era's favorite buzz as Ginsburg's was of his. Politically, the human rights movements of the 1700s (antimonarchical) and the 1900s (civil rights) both came to fruition as their associated pharmacies entered the mainstream. The coffee-crazed mobs of the French Revolution bear a certain resemblance to the pot-addled Vietnam War protesters of the 1960s. All this, by the way, is why American pundits should find consolation in the popularity of drugs like cocaine: despite their negative effects, it indicates Yanks still view getting wired as the preferred state of being. They should reserve their wails for the day when heroin and hot milk become the drugs of choice.

Drugs directly alter human behavior, productivity, and even reason. I'm not saying that medieval man was stupider than his modern cousin. He was merely decaffeinated and much like you or me before our first cup: grouchy and muddleheaded. It's also worth noting that the faults associated with alcohol (sloppy reasoning, credulity, and excessive emotion) were the vices of the medieval age, while the ills of excessive coffee drinking (overanalysis and short attention span) appear to plague our era. Some historians, however, have suggested that there is indeed a Precaffeinated Man, one physiologically distinct from *Homo coffea*. The renowned Wolfgang Schivelbush, in his book *Tastes of Paradise*, argues that the "massive, heavy body types typical of seventeenth-century paintings had their physiological explanation in high beer and beer soup consumption." The "insertion" of coffee, he continues, "achieved chemically... what the Protestants sought to fulfill spiritually" by "drying" up the beer-soaked bums and replacing them with "rationalistic, forward-looking bodies" typical of the lean cynics of the nineteenth century.

Ridiculous? Perhaps. If you really want ridiculous, though, try this one. Coffee and humanity both sprang from the same area in eastern Africa. What if some of those early ape-men nibbled on the bright red berries? What if the resulting mental stimulation opened them up to new ways of looking at old problems, much as it did Europeans? Could this group of berry nibblers be the Missing Link, and that memory of the bright but bitter-tasting fruit be the archetype for the story of the Garden of Eden?

Now *that's* ridiculous.

OF COURSE, NOT EVERYBODY AGREES WITH THE THESIS JUST outlined. A German sociologist of some sort had gone so far as to propose the exact opposite, that coffee caused the downfall of great civilizations. So from Vienna I took a train toward Germany.

First the Austrian police searched me, then the Germans. Peoples smell faded. Nobody smiled. It was all too typical.

The fact that this sociologist was stationed in Munich was no surprise. München is the home of the famous Oktoberfest, an annual get-together where thousands of beer lovers from all over the world (that means Australia) gather to drink themselves into a hysterical state of idiocy. It's the last great drinking festival from the medieval period and the perfect place for the last great anticoffee propagandist, Dr. Josef Joffe (pronounced "jof-fee").

"Ah, the Oktoberfest is an event," was Dr. Joffe's noncommittal comment. "But you have misunderstood my theory. I call it the Joffe Coffee Theory of Expansionism."

Joffe was a surprise on two counts. I'd expected some sort of crank. He turned out to be a trained sociologist and the head political editor of the German equivalent of *The New York Times*, the *Suddeutsche Zeitung*, a pleasantly bearish fellow who gave every appearance of enjoying the good things in life, including coffee, which his private secretary served immediately. So at the very least he was a well-paid crank.

Neither was his theory what I'd expected. It had come to him when, during a visit to Soviet Russia, he complained to his KGB handler about the awful coffee. The KGB dude replied that it was really the Kremlin's answer to America's neutron bomb—both killed people but left the buildings intact.

"It was then that I first saw this theory, this vision," said Joffe. "Bad coffee equals expansionism, imperialism, and war; good coffee drips with civility and pacifism and lassitude. I prove it. Quick—who makes the best coffee in the world?"

"The Italians?"

"And when was the last time the Italians won a war?"

"Hmm—what, A.D. 300?"

"And when did you Americans finally learn how to make coffee?"

"Oh, I guess in the sixties sometime."

"And when was the Vietnam War?"

"I see," I said. "Am I to understand that you're saying, for instance, that the current round of Chinese expansionism is the result of their inability to brew a decent cup of coffee?"

"Absolutely." He gestured to the window. "If we really wanted to end Chinese aggression today we would bomb them with Gaggia coffeemakers."

"Perhaps the UN peacemakers should carry Melita drips and Ethiopian Sidamo."

"Instead of machine guns? Precisely."

"What's the coffee like at the UN, do you know?"

He shook his head sadly. "It's not a pretty thought."

So his theory was pro-joe; or was it? His secretary brought in more coffee. Josef took a call. Maybe it was the sound of Josef speaking in German, a language so elegant and cruel, but something was bothering me. Dr. Joffe was clearly a lover of the cup, and his theory appeared to be the product of an enlightened mind. But when I pondered its parameters I saw the ominous truth: if bad coffee makes warmongers and good coffee creates wimps, all coffee, ipso facto, is evil.

It was, in fact, the old German anticoffee propaganda reborn. Germany has been the home for Europe's most voracious coffee haters since a ban issued by Frederick the Great in 1777. "It is disgusting to notice the increase in the quantity of coffee used by my subjects," he wrote. "Many battles have been fought and won by soldiers nourished by beer, and the king does not believe that coffee-drinking soldiers can be relied on." Bishops urged their congregations to destroy their coffee-making equipment. Frederick even hired wounded soldiers to roam the streets sniffing for the smell of roasting beans. These "coffee sniffers" were so successful that there came to be two types of coffee in Germany: "bean-coffee" (real coffee) and "coffee" (made from burnt bread, caramelized carrots, chicory, and God knows what else.)

"Yes, I remember that," said Joffe when he got off the phone. "We called it muck-fuck. Yes, yes, you pronounce it just like that, but you spell it mocha-faux. Means fake mocha. You must know the song that is sung to the musical notes of C-A-F-F-E-E? It goes '*Trink nicht so viel Caff-ee*' (Drink Not So Much Coffee). I think the tune is from a piece by Mozart."

Joffe's song is actually a remnant of yet a second antijava campaign which urged Germans to drink only chicory coffee because buying the real thing enriched "enemies" in France and Holland. Packages of chicory brew were decorated with labels showing a German peasant sowing chicory and waving away bags of coffee, under the caption "Healthy and Wealthy Without You."

It was so successful that Germany remained the sole decaffeinated and nondemocratic European power until World War I, two lacks that set the stage for the rise of the Nazis. It's worth noting that Hitler gained his following by speaking in bars, not cafés. To be fair, Gandhi, who was a vegetarian like Hitler, disapproved of coffee as well.

But we mustn't dwell on old wrongs. Germany has made amends and now serves some of the best coffee around.

"All this also proves my theory," said Joffe. "Before the war, Germans made the worst coffee in the world and, look, it got them all the way to Moscow! Since we learned how to make a cup, we have become as aggressive as sloths. Admittedly," he added, "this does not look good for America."

"I don't understand."

"America used to make atrocious coffee and great bombs. But since Starbucks they've been unable to win a war. If Starbucks expands unchecked, the Age of American greatness will end in an ocean of hazelnut and amaretto—you just don't fight with a Frappuccino in hand."

"This sounds fine, Joffe," I said, confronting him with my suspicions. "But if good coffee means decadence and bad coffee means war, how can coffee be anything but the devil's cup?"

"My friend, no, no, no." He shook his silver mane. "Ask yourself one question—is war a good thing?"

"Of course not," I murmured, taking another sip. "War is bad."

"Then good coffee is good." He unwrapped a cigarillo and lit up. "And bad coffee is bad. What could be more logical?"

"I like you, Joffe," I said. This was true. I mean, I didn't want to kiss him, but I might have sat in his lap. "Have you discussed this theory with other sociologists?"

"My colleagues would call my theory a specious correlation, but of course in sociology no one really knows what wags what."

Paris

I have tried to show the café as a place where one can go mad.

Vincent Van Gogh

My first stop, in Paris, was the central post office to pick up my forged Rajasthani paintings. I was an idiot. That was obvious to me, now that I was surrounded by serious-faced Frenchmen and their gray buildings. Not only had the whole art-smuggling conspiracy been a scam, but the existence of India herself—her neon colors, her ape-gods—seemed suspect. What had I been thinking about? What kind of brain-dead dolt would give two underage hustlers twelve hundred dollars for a bunch of day-glo doodling? Before entering the post office, I popped over to a nearby café to brace myself with a shot of something decidedly uncaffeinated. It was your typical Parisian joint, all brass and fake marble and people idling. Now, most Americans find it marvelous that the people of Paris can sit for days over a thimbleful of rocket fuel and fear no waiterly wrath. They don't realize that those people are not merely *sitting* in the chairs, they're *renting* them. It's not *joie de vivre* that keeps them there until cobwebs hang off their noses, it's miserliness. The entirety of twentieth-century philosophy is simply the result of penny-pinching Parisians falling prey to a dementia born of boredom, caffeine, and pomposity, the main symptoms of which are cubism, surrealism, and existentialism. All those earthshaking theories were nothing more than a desperate attempt to rationalize that extra ten-franc expenditure. You may, of course, stand at the *comptoir* for free, although then you must be willing to wallow in piles of discarded cigarette butts (it is against the law to have an ashtray at a Parisian *comptoir*—no one knows why).

I downed a quick calvados, standing, and headed over to the post office.

"No, *monsieur*, there is nothing." The man at the *poste restante* window was certain.

"But I don't understand why not," I said. "I even have insurance."

I waved my receipt at the clerk. It had never looked terribly official, even when I'd bought it in Jaipur. After three months in my money belt, it resembled a wisp of toilet paper.

"And what, may I ask, is this, *Monsieur*?"

"It's a receipt for the insurance," I said.

He peered at the slip.

"And what language, may I again ask, is this, *monsieur*?"

"It's a Hindu language. Urdu, I believe."

"I see." He handed it back. "You are now in France, *monsieur*. In France, we speak Freeench. And when, may I inquire, did you send the package?"

"Two months ago," I said. "You would think it would have arrived by now."

"Two months? Ahh, yes, it has undoubtedly arrived. However, you see, we only keep packages for three weeks. If they are not claimed by then, we send them back."

"Ahhh! But of course!" I was beginning to get into the swing of this fellow's repartee. "However, may I say, there was no return address on it. You could not, I think, therefore have sent it back, no? So it must, I would think, still be here, yes?"

"Not at all, *monsieur*," he smirked. "If there is no return address, the package is burned."

"Burned?" I was having trouble understanding his meaning. "With fire?"

"Exactly, *monsieur*."

I began to get excited. "Why, it was worth millions of...I don't know, certainly millions in some currency, somewhere. I must speak to a superior."

"You sent a package worth millions to *poste restante*? What, may I ask, was in the package?"

"Paintings. It was a big parcel with the market value and instructions to hold for three months. Are you sure there's no record?"

"May I ask what language the instructions were written in?"

"French."

"I see." He examined an enormous computer printout. "Well, apparently something from India arrived some time ago..." He hesitated. "Here, you must write your name and information."

It turned out there was a warehouse where they kept all the misaddressed, undeliverable, indecipherable, and unclaimed packets that the post office was too lazy to burn. If only I could get inside, I thought as I filled out the form. Who knew what I might find lying about. Van Gogh's ear. The bra of the lady on the twenty-franc note.

"Why don't you just give me the address and I'll go there myself," I suggested.

He shrugged. "As you like, *monsieur*. But it is four hundred kilometers from Paris."

IT'S ONE OF THE TRAVESTIES OF THE CAFFEINATED AGE THAT Europe's most celebrated cafés should serve some of the worst coffee. If Italian espresso is witty and rich, the French cup is bitter and oily. The Viennese like their cafés comfortable, spacious, replete with overstuffed chairs; Parisians prefer them crammed with doll-sized tables and chairs suitable for an interrogation chamber. Not to say that one is better than the other—the world is full of masochists—but it's fair to say they indicate different cultural priorities.

The Parisian café, for instance, is a clear manifestation of that nation's obsession with style. I do not say this lightly, and, indeed, I can prove it by returning to that pivotal decade of the 1670s. It was then, 1672 to be precise, that an Armenian named Pascal (said by some to be the same Pasqua who manned London's premier café twenty years earlier) opened the first Parisian establishment. Near St. Germain. It was a simple, honest café, utterly lacking in pretension and so, of course, of no interest to the French. It soon went out of business. Coffee remained "medicinal," and there it might have ended except that in this same decade the Turkish Ottomans were preparing their invasion of Vienna. One of their concerns was the possibility of

French interference, so they sent an ambassador named Solimon Aga to seduce Louis XIV into signing a nonaggression treaty.

Aga went to Paris and began his wooing. For six months he invited Paris's *crème de la crème*, one by one, up to his apartments to chat and, in the Turkish tradition, share coffee. The drink, as I've said, had been seen in Paris. But not like this. Guests were received in chambers hung with priceless Turkish carpets. Before taking coffee, they were washed with rosewater. Then their heads were enclosed in a silk tent under which myrrh was burned to perfume their faces. Finally an African *kahvedjibachi* in gorgeous costume would roast, pound, and brew the mysterious "black wine" and, according to Isaac D'Israeli, "on bended knee serve the choicest mocha...poured out in saucers of gold and silver, placed on embroidered silk dollies fringed with gold bouillon."

It was too exotic to resist, and invitations to Soliman's little *tête-à-têtes* were soon the most desirable in town. Louis, who had refused to see the ambassador, finally invited Soliman to drop by the palace. The meeting quickly became a fashion showdown, French Rococo against Turkish mystique. Louis had a robe worth fourteen million livres (approximately thirty million dollars) made for the occasion. He had a reception hall decorated with massive silver furniture and surrounded himself with hundreds of courtiers. Soliman appeared almost alone, wearing simple robes. The only thing truly precious was his coffee service—solid gold *ibriks*, diamond studded *zarfs*, rarely seen Chinese porcelain.

Soliman won, and anybody who was anybody soon had a room decorated à la Turk where, dressed in Arabic duds and served by a Nubian slave, they would sit and sip mocha, a fad that Molière would immortalize in *Le Bourgeois Gentilhomme*:

MSSR. JOURDAIN: *(Entering with a huge turban on his head)*

Mamamouchi, I tell you. I am a Mamamouchi!

MME. JOURDAIN: *What beast is that?*

MSSR. JOURDAIN: *In your language, a Turk.*

MME. JOURDAIN: *A Turk? Are you of an age to be a Moorish dancer?*

Louis signed the treaty, and within a decade Vienna was surrounded by three-hundred thousand Turks. The Turks lost, and the Paris coffee fad began to fade. Then, three years after the siege of Vienna, a Sicilian named Francesco Procopio dei Coltelli opened a place called Café Procope. Procope, however, had learned a lesson from the Turkish ambassador's success. He had realized that it was not coffee the drink that interested the French, but coffee the fashion statement. Where the earlier Parisian cafés had been down to earth, Café Procope was royal. It had marble tables and mirrors and chandeliers. There were waiters in powdered wigs. There were Turkish sherbets and liqueurs. The Sicilian had created a Disneyfied version of a nobleman's coffee salon, right down to the condescending footmen. The French melted like butter. Voltaire became a regular, as did Napoleon, Rousseau, D'Alembert and, today, any number of tourists wearing short pants and Mickey Mouse caps. The success of Café Procope (on and off for three hundred years) ensured that it became the archetype of Parisian cafés, where the emphasis remains on being seen in grand surroundings.

The reason was that the French did not actually like the taste of the Turks' "bitter wine," an aversion that supposedly led to the introduction of sugar by the Turkish ambassador. "There are two things Frenchmen will never swallow," wrote Madame de Sevigné in the 1670s, "coffee and Racine's poetry." The Duchess of Orléans compared coffee to soot. Louis XIV thought it vile. That being said, no matter how much the royals disliked the stuff they were doubtless deeply moved by its unique ability, in the words of sixteenth-century coffee scholar Paludanus, to "breaketh wind and openeth any stopping." This was coffee's first claim to fame in Europe,[1] most poignantly as an *electuary* of melted butter, salt, honey, and coffee, which one took after inserting a *provang* (a three-foot-long whale bone) down one's throat and into the stomach. The French did not *provang* but they were obsessed with the issue of "stoppings." Voltaire himself dedicated a whole section of his *Dictionnaire philosophique* (supposedly conceived in a café) to the topic, and the king was so gravely afflicted that his dining chair was modified to double as a toilet to ensure no opportunity passed unexploited. One of Versailles' most prestigious positions was *Gentilhomme porte Coton*, a man who, armed with little more than a cotton ball and a silver platter, would receive the Sun King's tragically infrequent droppings and hurry them to the appropriate authority.

This ancient tradition explains not only the French use of espresso as an after-dinner digestive but also sheds some light on the inexplicably awful nature of the national cup. First the bean itself. The French drink about 50 percent of the Robusta beans in Europe. Robustas, while lower in quality, are particularly caffeinated. Caffeine causes the muscle spasms associated with "unblockings." This natural attribute is amplified by the "French roast," in which the bean is burnt beyond recognition, thus enhancing carbon and oil content. Carbon absorbs gastric gases, facilitating traffic flow; fats and oils are known laxatives.

SINCE IT WOULD TAKE THE POSTAL SERVICE AT LEAST TWO WEEKS to figure out where they'd put my paintings, and since Paris is so obscenely expensive, I decided to try to find some casual

[1] Our friend was also credited with curing miscarriages, headaches, rheumatism, consumption, scurvy, gout, dropsy, kidney stones, eye sores, and, of course, the common cold. But it was particularly popular as a digestive aid.

work. I'd worked in Paris during the late 1980s, typing novels and washing dishes, but this time I wanted to work as a *café garçon*, a waiter. In the days of Procope, waiters doubled as in-house encyclopedias who, having personally heard Voltaire's latest pronouncement, could be counted on to authoritatively settle any dispute. It's still a prestigious position, in a way. The city's finest compete every year to see who can run the fastest hundred meters while balancing a tray of *café crèmes*. At the very least you get to wear tight pants and sneer at tourists, two pastimes no Frenchman can long resist.

I thought my best chance would be among the Greek cafés in the Latin Quarter, and after a day of wandering its cobblestone alleys, I actually received an offer of sorts. It was a little café-restaurant with that look of dusty contentment that comes only to places unmolested by customers. The manager, a nattily dressed Syrian, greeted me like an old friend. As he led me back to his office, I noticed that the kitchen was stacked with unwashed dishes. There seemed to be no other employees. We chatted about my experience (limited) and working papers (forged). Then he asked me if I was a member of the dishwashers' union.

"Well, hmm," I said. I wasn't sure I'd understood him. A dishwashers' union? Was there really such a thing? "Actually, I was looking for a position as a waiter."

He shrugged. "There is no difference."

"No difference?"

"It is the same."

I was getting it. The piles of unwashed dishes, the lack of visible staff. "I would be doing both, yes?"

"Of course," he said. "You mentioned you had experience as a cook."

"Yes, but—"

"But you are not a member of the dishwashers' union? I'm afraid I can't let you work unless you are in the union. They are very strict."

"The strictest," I agreed, standing up. "I will go see my friend immediately. He can help, I am sure."

The friend I referred to was Moussa, a gentleman from Mali with whom I'd worked during the eighties. Those were the Roaring Eighties, when Ronald Reagan's rape of the American economy sent the dollar sky high and made Paris almost affordable for Yank expats like myself. Bless his soul! For fifty cents I'd been able to feign profundity at the Parisian café of my choice. A glass of red had cost under a dollar. Rent on my river barge just opposite the Louvre was less than seventy-five dollars a month. The fact that I woke up with icicles over my head and "flushed" my toilet by tossing it overboard, or that my job paid $2.50 an hour, was irrelevant at those prices. Moussa was a dishwasher (now chef), and I felt sure that if anybody could get me into the dishwashers' union, he could. He's a wonderful man—kind, bawdy, an old-fashioned country gentleman from the sub-Sahara with a little girl's giggle and a Pinocchio nose. Fond of holding hands. Nothing would give me greater pleasure than to expound at length about Moussa. A rare and wonderful person. Unfortunately, he was useless.

"A dishwashers' union?" he said. "That's ridiculous! He must have been drunk."

I next looked up Monsieur François Bailtrand, a retired union judge who lives in the ground-floor *chambre* of his family's hotel. A small man, perhaps eighty, with a stutter and lilac-tinted teeth.

"Ah, Monsieur, you know it is not so easy, even for most Frenchmen," he said, when I found him. "To work in the cafés you really need to be an Auvergnat. I believe they still are the dominant tribe of the cafés."

"There's a café tribe?" I said. "You mean a caste, like in India?"

"What, you mean you do not know the story of the Auvergnats? They are the fathers of the Parisian café." He pulled down some books from the shelves lining the walls of his bed/dining room. "They are, you know, a tribe or a very large family. Not a caste. But my family, too, is from Auvergne."

"Your family ran a café?"

"This was a café, here where you sit. Back then—hotel, café—it was all the same."

Auvergne is a mountainous region five hundred miles or so south of Paris. Today it's popular for horseback riding. Back in the 1700s, it was a poverty-stricken backwater peopled by peasants who scratched out a living as coal miners. Auvergnats, as the people from the region are called, were and are famous for their stubborn independence and are supposed to be descended from the Ukrainians. According to Monsieur Balitrand, they appeared in Paris selling their villages' coal as *charbonniers* (hence the nickname Charbougnats). They then started peddling water and lemonade, then hot water, which they boiled using the coal they also sold. When coffee came into vogue they brewed it to order on people's doorsteps, a Parisian tradition that goes back to a crippled boy called Le Candiot who sold coffee door-to-door in the late 1600s.

Dragging all this stuff about the muddy streets of Paris became a nuisance. So one by one the Auvergnats picked a spot and set up shop. Walls grew around their carts. They stuck a chair or two outside. Occasionally someone even washed a dish. And so Deux Magot, Café Flore, Lipp, and a zillion other famous Parisian cafés came into being. By the late 1800s about half a million Auvergnats had moved to the city. To this day they remain a tribe apart, with special newspapers and soirées that reunite entire villages.

Among the early arrivals had been Monsieur Balitrand's great-great-great-great-great-great-grandfather from the village of St. Come d'Olt in northern Auvergne.

"We chose this spot in the late 1800s," said Monsieur Balitrand of his Hotel Henry IV, an ancient maze of a place on L'Ile de la Cité. "I would say that maybe fifty percent of the people in my family's village opened cafés or hotels here."

By the mid-1700s, these establishments (Auvergne and pre-Auvergne) had turned Paris into "one vast café," according to Jules Michelet. Like their British brethren, French cafés were heavily involved in the political reforms of the time. What's absolutely fascinating is the different ways the two institutions approached the situation. English coffeehouses featured sober, serious discussion and debate. The cafés of Paris turned political reform into a theatrical experience. The infamous Café des Aveugles featured a blind orchestra led by a deaf singer as a parody of the incompetent royal government. Its neighbor, Café Vert, boasted a monkey trained to leap at the throat of any customer denounced as an aristocrat. Frivolous, cruel, sarcastic: terribly Parisian.

By the 1780s, however, things started getting serious. "The coffeehouses of Palais Royal," wrote English traveler Arthur Young in 1789, "present the most astonishing spectacle, crowded within and without by crowds listening to [impromptu] speeches.... The thunder of applause [with which] they receive every sentiment of violence against the present government cannot be easily imagined."

It was at the cafés of the Palais Royal that, on July 12, 1789, Camille Desmoulins leaped upon a table and urged the mob to take up arms against the aristocracy. It had been done a million times before, but this time, after a debate over what the most appropriate color for the revolution would be (green for renewal or red for blood?), the café's customers actually got out of their seats, went outside, and overthrew the French monarchy, incidentally ending government as it was then known.

Some social critics of the time portrayed coffee as the stimulant that helped set off both the Enlightenment and Europe's first democratic revolution. "For this sparkling outburst," wrote Michelet, "there is no doubt that honor should be ascribed in part to the great event which created new customs and even modified human temperament—the advent of coffee...which brings forth the sparkle and sunlight of truth."[2] Historian Narcisse-Achille Salvandy put it in black and white: "No government can go against the sentiment of the cafés. The Revolution took place because they were for the Revolution. Napoleon reigned because they were for glory."

Pretty enough stuff, and perhaps even true. But there is another less celebrated role that Old Man Java played in the July revolution, one that again takes us deep within the Gallic digestive system: to wit, that belonging to the notorious Marquis de Sade. At the time, our dear marquis was imprisoned in the Bastille. On July 2, ten days before Desmoulins hopped on his table at Café Foy, the marquis had done a little rabble-rousing himself. Following a disagreement with his jailer, he'd grabbed the funnel used to empty his chamber pot into the moat and, using it as a megaphone, had started screaming out his cell window that the government was "cutting the prisoner's throats" in the Bastille. A crowd gathered outside. As the prison guards

---

[2] Michelet goes so far as to categorize the French Enlightenment by the changing coffee supply. When the lighter beans of Yemen were available, the lighthearted cafés and salons of the aristos dominated. The medium-strength bean of Bourbon brought on the "sparkling verse of Voltaire." When the "full, coarse" coffees of the Caribbean became the norm, the age turned dark and violent.

struggled to open his cell door, the marquis urged the mob to rescue the "political prisoners" locked within. Then the guards subdued him.

Historians have long puzzled over why the revolutionaries stormed the Bastille. Everyone knew it held only a few imprisoned aristocrats, like the Marquis de Sade. Well, it appears that within hours of the marquis's outburst rumors spread that the government had moved all its political detainees into the Bastille and was slitting their throats. The rumors grew. Ten days later the fortress was stormed. The rebels found no political prisoners. In fact, there were only three captives in the entire place. They did, however, stumble upon a huge cache of weapons, without which, it is generally agreed, the French Revolution would have failed.

But what had the marquis been so outraged about? It was those old "unblocking" problems again. After twelve years of being locked up, the marquis was corked tight as a bottle of Dom Perignon, "puffy, overweight and suffering formidable gastritis," according to *Sade*, the definitive biography by Maurice Levenger. He constantly demanded "appropriate" breakfasts and grew furious when Lossinoette, "the dirtiest and most insolent of valets," took away his "rump cushion." Coffee, of course, was famous for its prowess in these areas, and though the records of his coffee-drinking habits are sketchy, there's little doubt that its lack, played a key role in his intestinal distress. His cries of torment were without a doubt what eventually drew the mobs to the Bastille on July 14, 1789.

IT WAS ALL DOWNHILL FROM THERE, AS WE GET INTO WHAT some fools call the Golden Age of the French café. You know the cast. There was our old friend Arthur Rimbaud, the coffee merchant cum poet of Harrar, who used to hang out with that icon of decadent café society, Paul Verlaine, at Café Rat Mort. These two were the Sid Vicious and Johnny Rotten of the 1800s. Rimbaud asks Verlaine to put his hands on the table and then slits the man's wrists; Verlaine returns the compliment by shooting Rimbaud. That kind of thing. Later, there were the existentialists like Sartre and Camus at Café Flore, the Americans at Café Lipp and La Coupole, cubists like Picasso at Le Lapin Agile, dadaist Guillame Apollinaire and surrealist André Breton at the Rotonde. There was even a group called Incoherents at Le Café des Incoherent. People like Alexandre Schanne and Henri Murger made a career doing exposés on "*les cafés decadent*." The owner of Café Momu complained that "our waiter was reduced to an idiot in the prime of his life, as a result of the conversations he had to listen to."

As fond as I am of these lounge lizards, I have to point out that they only talked a revolution. Desmoulins and his crew at the Palais Royal threw one.

No, the most significant legacy of this lot stems from their Herculean efforts to stretch a single espresso twelve hours. Sartre, in particular, has much to atone for in this area. According to the proprietor of Café Flore, Paul Boulal, our lofty existentialist was "the most awful client...sitting from morning to night over a single drink that was never refilled." Thanks to such behavior, the world's café capital is now the most expensive place in the world to sit and enjoy a cup—up to seven U.S. dollars, compared to Vienna's four or Amsterdam's two. Small wonder that the French are avoiding cafés like the plague. In 1960 Paris boasted 252,000 small cafés. By 1982 there were about 180,000, a number that has now decreased almost 50 percent. Another 6,000 are expected to close this year. Old favorites disappear each visit.

"Oh, yes, it is all changed," agreed Monsieur Balitrand. "For many reasons—McDo [McDonald's] and the fast food is so popular. But there have always been cafés, and they will always be here. Really, they are the history of the French people."

the Sultan's Earache

At breakfast Beethoven drank coffee, which he usually prepared himself in a percolator. Coffee seems to have been the nourishment with which he could least dispense and in his procedure with regard to its preparation he was as careful as the Orientals are known to be. Sixty beans to a cup was the allotment and the beans were often counted out exactly, especially when guests were present.

Anton Schindler

BEHIND THE EXPLOSIVE growth in Europe's coffee consumption during the 1700s lay the tedious principle of supply and demand. In the late 1600s Louis XV reportedly spent the equivalent of fifteen thousand dollars a year to feed his daughter's coffee habit. By 1740 the price had dropped to fifty cents a cup, and even the lowliest of lumpens could afford a buzz. Coffee was now flourishing in European colonies on three different continents. The first major transplant had been Baba

Budan's legendary smuggling of the bean to India. A more important one came in 1616, when a Dutch sea captain named Pieter Van Der Broecke stole a dozen plants from Mocha and planted them in Java, thus changing coffee's nickname from mocha to mocha-java. But by far the pivotal feat of these colonial drug cartels was the smuggling of the bean to the New World by a French aristocrat named Gabriel De Clieu in 1720.

When I read De Clieu's story in Paris I was instantly reminded of the Viennese spy Kolschitzky. It was as unlikely as a Tom Clancy novel, so full of pirates and spies and shipwrecks that it couldn't possibly be true. A quick bit of research showed that De Clieu's claim rested largely on a letter he himself wrote in 1774. A little more digging turned up any number of counterclaims, including the unlikely story of a French doctor who was supposedly given sixty coffee plants for having cured the sultan of Yemen's earache. There were also accounts of the Dutch planting coffee in Surinam, South America, in 1714, six years before De Clieu, as well as the story of a Portuguese officer who was given a bouquet of coffee flowers after servicing an adulterous French countess. Our old friends the Capuchin monks had even staked a claim.

What it came down to was that nobody knew how the plant had arrived in the New World, and De Clieu had been given credit because he had cooked up the best story. I tried to find out more about the French sailor, but after a week of poking about the French National Library, I knew only that De Clieu had been born in a town called Anglequeville around 1686. He later became governor of Guadeloupe. No one, however, knew where he was buried. When I tried to track down Anglequeville, I discovered there was no such place. My only clue I had was that Anglequeville had been located in the state of Seine-Inferieure, on the French North Atlantic coast near Normandy.

I needed to find out if De Clieu's claim was valid, so when it became clear that the French postal service was never going to find my Rajasthani paintings, I grabbed a train heading for Normandy. It was a lovely ride. Green hills dotted with cream-colored sheep. Apple trees heavy with fruit. Oddly autumnal, I thought, as the train whizzed along, but nice. The city of Rouen went by. Then a place called Auffay. Then Longueville-sur-Scie, Malanvay L'Home, and Victoire L'Abbaye. Funny how the smaller the village, the longer the name. We were now in Seine-Inferieure. Still no sign of Anglequeville. I noticed a sea tang in the air, and the train came to a halt. End of the line, Dieppe. I found a cheap room above a bar and started to explore.

My method was not quite as idiotic as it sounds. True, I had no idea where Anglequeville was located, but the name suggested a contraction of Anglais Ville, "English Town." Since De Clieu was a sailor and lived in a town associated with England, it almost had to be one of Seine-Inferieure's ports, of which there are only twenty or so. All I had to do was go from port to port and barhop until I found someone who had heard of the family.

Dieppe proved to be a delightfully small Norman fishing village. People were grilling herrings on the street. There was a little market by the church. Everybody was over forty-five and tipsy.

"*Le poisson pêche,*" a man in blue overalls was muttering at my first research stop, a harborside bar called Café Le Crystal. "*Alors, nous pêchons les pêchons, pêchons on frères, non? Nous sommes tout les pecheurs.*" This roughly translates as, "The fish fish; we fish. Therefore the fish are our brothers because we are both fisherman, no?"

I ordered a beer.

"Fish the fish," continued the man, apparently addressing me. "Don't you see? If the fish fish for fish, they are fishermen, ah? So we fish for fishermen. But we are fishermen too! So we are eating our own brothers, eh?"

"Ooh là là," interjected the twitchy blonde behind the bar. "Not at all. Fish who eat fish are cannibals. So if we kill cannibals, what's so wrong with that, eh? Cannibals are disgusting and deserve to die."

"Besides, my friend," said a bald fellow in a leather jacket, "a fish who fishes for fish is not a fisher*man*; he is a fisher*fish*. Totally different."

"No. Those who fish the sea are all brothers, no matter what," said Blue Overalls. "If a policeman eats another policeman, is he not a cannibal?"

Bald took a sip of his beer. "Not if the other policeman is a pig, he's not."

This caused a pause. I asked if anybody had heard of a De Clieu or Anglequeville.

"Ask the fish," said Overalls. "They know everything."

"De Clieu?" repeated the bartender. "No, never."

"It's an old name," I persisted. "I'm not sure—"

"I don't know," she snapped suddenly. "Thank you, sir, and good-bye."

Someone put a hand on my shoulder. It was Baldie. "Look, *mon ami*, I don't know of a family named De Clieu," he said. "But there is an Avenue De Clieu down by the train station. Perhaps they live there."

I went back down to the station, and there it was, nailed to the wall of a pharmacy. Avenue De Clieu. I celebrated my luck with a meal at a tacky harbor restaurant. Sautéed flounder with *frites*, salmon pâté, crème caramel. I chatted with the waitress about the book I was reading. ("Ah, yes, I know this P. G. Wodehouse".) After a few glasses of white wine I decided to marry her. We would live in Dieppe. Like everyone else, I would fish the sea. In the summer, the tourists would come. Gigot and I would have many children, many, and they would have children of their own and so on and so on and so on.

"YES, YES, I AM GABRIEL DE CLIEU'S GREAT-GREAT-GREAT-GREAT-great-great-great-granddaughter." Madame Catherine de Beaunay-Cotelle started counting on her fingers. "I am not sure, there might be one more."

By an amazing stroke of luck, Dieppe was not only where De Clieu had been born,[1] it also contained his sole direct descendant, this middle-aged, no-nonsense French lady shod in black-and-white wingtips. The day after I arrived in Dieppe she had picked me up at a café and chauffeured me to her office in the neighboring village of Derchigny-Graincourt, where for the last three years she had been documenting her ancestor's feat.

"No, there is no question who carried the plant," she said, bringing out a pile of papers. "It is historically proven fact. There is even a book written on the subject."

Catherine handed me a slender yellow volume entitled *Gabriel De Clieu: Hommage au chevalier*. It was written by Catherine de Beaunay-Cotelle.

"But you wrote this!" I objected.

"Of course. Who would better know than his only descendant?"

She had a point. She also had letters attesting to De Clieu's feat from Louis XV, the governor of Martinique, various colonial bureaucrats, and an American biologist who'd named an entire species of the coffee plant after De Clieu. She even had a copy of De Clieu's coat of arms, an eagle, beak open in a battle cry, on a field of silver and crowned with three grains of sand. I told her

[1] Dieppe's significant role in coffee's history might explain why it is traditional here to toast weddings and baptisms with coffee and not wine.

she looked a bit like the old chevalier, a portrait of whom adorned the front of her book. He was an old white guy in a wig with sea-gray eyes. Genial, but not the kind of grandfather you want to play pranks on. Actually, Catherine seemend pretty sober herself.

"It is something I am very passionate about," she said, observing my glance. She definitely had the chevalier's eyes. "It has become my life's work."

Aside from documenting De Clieu's voyage to the New World, she was trying to open a museum on coffee's role in French history. She had recently formed the Association De Clieu (I am its 251st member) and convinced seventeen nearby villages to buy the chevalier's abandoned château to house her museum.

According to Catherine, her family was made part of the aristocracy by Charles VI. Gabriel was born in Dieppe around 1687 and joined the navy around 1702. For the next fifteen years he'd lounged about the French Caribbean, winning various honors, getting married, but essentially being a bum. Around 1717 he apparently heard about a Michel Isambert who had perished trying to transplant three coffee plants to the Antilles. Gabriel took up the cause, succeeded, and was rewarded with the governership of Guadeloupe and by being made Commander of the Order of St. Louis, not to mention the hero of coffee lovers everywhere.

"He died poor, in Paris, despite having been the governor," she said. "But he was a good governor, they say. When he was poor, the people of Guadeloupe offered to send him a hundred and fifty thousand livres [francs]. He refused, of course."

"But he still owned land here?"

"Oh yes. His family's descendants today control about eighty hectares all around us. Yet he died destitute. It was typical of the time after the Revolution." She put away her notes. "But there is no question about my ancestor's gift to the world. Think about it! That one man should have brought so much happiness."

"Yes, amazing." I paused, unsure how to express my skepticism. "The story, you know, of the voyage. It seems so incredible. Is it true?"

"Ah, it is amazing, no? Come." She led me to a large building filled with flowers. "You see?" she said, gesturing to the plants. I looked around in puzzlement. Then I saw it, behind the ferns and flowers, a huge mural depicting De Clieu's odyssey. There were the pirates and mermaids, and sailors dying of thirst. There was a terrible storm. The last panel showed the paradise of Martinique, where De Clieu's wife, a monkey on her lap, was being served a cup of coffee by an African slave. The colors were beginning to fade.

"It was his destiny, you see," she said. "I had his horoscope drawn. He was born in the house of Saturn, indicating perseverance, and Mercury, which means long voyages. His sign in the Thebaique calendar is of a man with a basket in his right hand and seeds in his left. It means, they say, he was destined to sow great seeds across the world."

"What sign was he?" I asked.

"We think he was born June 30, 1687. Sign of Cancer."

"Really? That's my sign."

"Ah, you know, I don't completely believe in these things," she scoffed. "But if you are going to take the same route as my ancestor, you should be sure to bring some bottled water."

ACCORDING TO CATHERINE COTELLE, DE CLIEU SET SAIL SOME twenty miles south of Dieppe, in Rochefort. When I went there to arrange passage on a freighter, however, there was nothing available. In fact, working for passage on commercial freighters is a thing of the past, at least in Europe, where freighters are booked in advance. The only vessel I could find was a tramp ship leaving from the northern Italian port of Genoa. And I would have to pay; not much, but it would have to be cash, and they would not guarantee a date of departure. Nor was it going to Martinique, but to the famous Brazilian coffee port of Santos.

The next few weeks were rather complicated. So I won't mention the day that I arrived in Genoa to discover that my freighter, the *SS Venezia*, was delayed. Nor shall I tell of the day the authorities changed the date of departure three times in twenty-four hours. Neither shall I detail the weeks I spent idling about Rome and Naples; the countless Cellinis, the endless Michelangelos, the pre-Raphaelites, the post-Raphaelites, and the pre-post-but-indisposed Raphaelites. Let us instead proceed to the day four weeks later when I again stood upon the docks of Genoa waiting to board. It wasn't the *SS Venezia*, which had mysteriously disappeared, but the *SS Pisa*. Same difference. As long as it floated I could not have cared less.

Writers tend to portray docks as romantic, mysterious places, and perhaps they once were. The modern ones, however, more closely resemble parking lots, and the ships, skyscrapers. The *SS Pisa* measured almost two hundred yards long and floated five stories high (there were an additional six below sea level). The dock was littered with huge steel boxes painted primary blues and reds. To load sixty thousand pounds of coffee in the 1800s required three hundred trips by a stevedore with two hundred pounds on his shoulder. Today it's done in one trip by a single man hidden in a crane.

The only people in sight that day were my fellow passengers, eight in total, most in their early seventies. No one spoke English. After two hours, a crew member led us into the ship's hold. We were shipping tractors. An Italian man with false teeth made me promise to sit at his dinner table. Then we were led to our cabins. Everything was painted flat blue. As I began to unpack, the baby down the hall began screaming. A huge crash came from below.

INTRODUCING NONNATIVE PLANT SPECIES TO DIFFERENT PARTS OF the world was among the most significant activities of the early European explorers. They originally concentrated on bringing New World exotica, like tomatoes, to Europe. Sugar from Africa to Brazil was the first major transplant from the Old World to the New. Coffee was second. There appear to have been two or three earlier attempts to plant coffee in the Western Hemisphere, one possibly by De Clieu himself. Whatever the case, by the time he approached Louis XV for a pair of plants, the king was unenthused. This Louis loved coffee. He personally harvested, roasted, and brewed his cup with beans from the garden (acquired from the mayor of Amsterdam, they were direct descendants of the plants smuggled out of Mocha a century earlier), and his coffee-roasting soirées with his royal mistress Madame Du Barry were something of a scandal.

"I made many trips in my attempts to obtain a sprig of a coffee plant from the royal garden, where they had been kept for some years," wrote De Clieu. "I returned over and over without success." After months of waiting, De Clieu finally got smart and employed "a lady of quality" to entreat the royal physician, Monsieur De Chirac, to hand over some buds. The name and skills of the lady are unknown, but in the fall of 1720 the doctor sent two seedlings to the garden in Rochefort to acclimatize themselves to the sea air. On October 8 they were loaded onto a ship appropriately named *Le Dromedaire*, "the Camel," and set sail for the West.

At Sea

The discovery of coffee was, in its way, as important as the invention of the telescope or of the microscope... For coffee has unexpectedly intensified and modified the capacities and activities of the human brain.

Heinrich Eduard Jacob

SEA VOYAGES AND PRISON terms have a number of characteristics in common. There is no escape. Meals are served at fixed times. The food is awful. You have no choice about whose company you keep. All the passengers on the SS *Pisa* took their meals together at three side-by-side tables. The first table was dominated by a Swiss biologist named Christian, his Brazilian wife, and their three-year-old daughter. Another table held an older Italian couple, a seventy-nine-year-old French-Swiss woman named Jacqueline, and her admirer, Bruno. I shared a table with two Italian men, Sergio and Franco. Meals were chaos. The engine's vibrations made our chairs crawl away from the table, and it was so loud we had to yell. The food, if not too good, was plentiful: first a huge bowl of pasta, then a fish, then a meat, then a vegetable, and finally a rancid orange. The wine came from cardboard cartons. The coffee was unspeakable.

"*Bellissimo!*" exclaimed my table companion Sergio at the first dinner. "I love this bread! Don't you love it? Isn't this the best bread? It's the best bread. I love the sailing life. Ahhhhhhh!"

Sergio was a handsome old man with slicked-down gray hair and pale eyes. Supposedly quite charming, if you spoke his language, as a dining companion, he left a little to be desired. If he didn't care for whatever he was eating, he simply spat it out, discreetly wrapping it in his beloved bread rolls. By the end of every meal there was a pile of half-chewed meat-and-bread wads decorating his plate. He was also a tan fan and by the end of the voyage had burned himself a bright pink. His eyes were permanently bloodshot.

That first night, though, he seemed all right. Definitely upbeat. He loved the bread, the food, the sea, the Brazilian girls. Everything was wonderful!

"I am speaking before the rotary club of São Paulo," he bragged.

"The rotary club?" I teased. "Isn't that part of the Mafia?"

He grew suddenly serious. "We don't discuss the Mafia at dinner."

I was to discover that Italians never discuss controversial subjects at meals. The pope was out. So was the secession of northern Italy. European union was *verboten*. Ditto for Mussolini. It all upset the digestion, although, considering the food we were eating, it seemed a lost cause.

Fortunately, we had Sergio to find a silver lining in everything, including my destination.

"Santos! You are going to Santos? The coffee port? You are a lucky man. The route has changed. Santos is now the *last* stop." He paused to spit out another mouthful of half-chewed veal. "You will have six weeks to enjoy the sea and delicious food."

"Six weeks? I thought it was supposed to take fourteen days."

"Not any more." He leaned forward conspiratorially. "But you don't have to pay a penny extra. The captain told us today at the meeting. Didn't you listen?"

"Is that what he was talking about?" I felt like throwing up. "My Italian is not so good."

Sergio nodded happily. "Ahh, it must be a pleasant surprise."

The *SS Pisa* crawled across the Ligurian Sea and then down Spain's Costa Brava, stopping only at Valencia, where I spent the afternoon watching eighty-year-old drunken sailors scream songs in a local bar.

We entered the Strait of Gibraltar. The strait is the sole connection between the Mediterranean and the Atlantic, and once through we'd be in a real ocean. The thought mortified me (I have a horror of becoming seasick), so I took a double dose of Dramamine that night. I awoke at four in the morning to find my cabin doing somersaults. Bottles fell, books tumbled. I downed some more Dramamine and passed out again.

The sea was calm when I awoke. Africa was pouring by to starboard, but haze kept the continent invisible. Around sunset I saw some Moroccan fishing boats. One that appeared just at dusk struck me as odd. It flew no flag. No crew was visible, nor were there any fishing nets. I was sitting in the prow when it cut across our bow, with only fifty yards to spare, so I got a pretty good look at it before it disappeared into the night.

At dinner I asked Captain Vitello, a string bean of a man who seemed more maître d' than sailor, if he thought the ship I'd seen might have been a Moroccan pirate checking us out.

"No, no." He gave me one of his trademark I'm-about-to-have-a-nervous-breakdown smiles. "Not here. In a few days maybe there will be pirates."

"Tomorrow? We have pirates tomorrow?"

"Perhaps. Nigeria has pirates. And Togo."

Modern pirates prefer to pick on private yachts. But in De Clieu's day they went after everybody. In fact, everybody was a pirate, and even the most respectable of captains made an occasional raid. Buccaneers caught up with De Clieu's ship a few weeks after they'd set sail. De Clieu claims they were Tunisians who struck during a dead calm in the middle of the night. Fortunately, the *Dromedaire*'s twenty-six cannons convinced them to look elsewhere.

We did not have the luck to be raided by pirates. No pirates, no whales, not even the sight of land. We sailed past Morocco, then mysterious Mauritania, and then the almost legendary country known as Western Sahara, one of the few places on earth lacking any form of government. If only we were on the *Qasid Karin*, my boat to Yemen, I thought over and over. We would doubtless get shipwrecked and be able to do some exploring. The *Pisa*, however, just kept plodding ahead at fifteen miles an hour.

The problem with the *SS Pisa*, at least from my point of view, was that it was neither uncomfortable enough to qualify as an adventure nor luxurious enough to be a pleasure.

"Oh, but last time it was so different," replied the elderly French-Swiss woman, Jacqueline, when I mentioned my qualms one morning. "There was music and dancing all night. Why, there was a concert violinist among the passengers, and every night he would come to my cabin and play for me."

I'd begun lingering over my morning coffee and *panetonne* with Christian, the boyish Swiss biologist, and Jacqueline. Jacqueline was a sweet old lady, always dressed in a faded sweater and flowered head scarf. I quite liked her and admired her gumption in traveling alone at her age.

"Ah, Jacqueline," I teased, "is the violin the only instrument he played in your room?"

"Ahhh, Stew-ar!" she tittered. Then she moaned. "But it is no funny thing when you get old like me, traveling by yourself."

I impolitely agreed. "Yes, it does get harder to travel with age."

Christian came to her rescue. "No! I think it is marvelous that you get out and travel, Jacqueline! You should!"

"But of course," she said. "What, now that I have had the children and raised the family, I should stay home and cook the spaghetti?" She mimed stirring a pot with a doleful expression. "No! Never! I want to go out and see the world and learn, eh? Traveling opens your eyes, *non*? What, I should stay in the cellar and become another moldy potato?"

"Not at all," I agreed. "Not another moldy potato, please."

"I shall go and visit my friend in Recife," she said. Recife is an old port town in northern Brazil. "He is such a dear friend."

"More than Bruno?" I teased. I had noticed our fellow passenger, a red-faced Italian, making goo-goo eyes at her.

"Oh! Bruno!" She laughed. "Speak of moldy potatoes!"

HAVING SURVIVED THE TUNISIAN PIRATES, DE CLIEU BECAME AWARE that the Dutch government had planted a spy on board the *Dromedaire*. Dutch colonies in Java were beginning to produce large quantities of the bean, and they, like the Arabs before them, were going to great lengths to maintain their monopoly. Unfortunately, very little is known about the spy. De Clieu modestly shrugs aside this early case of international economic espionage by saying, "It is useless to recount the difficulties I had in saving my delicate plant from the hands of a man who, basely jealous of the joy I was about to taste through being of service to my country," attempted to destroy the seedlings.

It appears that the spy's attempts to uproot De Clieu's treasures forced the Frenchman to sit with the plants by day and lock them in his cabin at night. The Dutchman might very well have succeeded if it hadn't been for the special containers De Clieu had constructed for transporting his protégés. Prior to De Clieu, plants had been transported in baskets covered with a reed cage, allowing limited light and also exposing the plants to a great deal of corrosive sea air. De Clieu built the first portable glasshouse, essentially a wooden box sealed with wire and a glass front. The wire kept rats out and let air in, while the glass preserved the day's heat. It became the model container for moving plants by sea. For this voyage, it also hindered the Dutch spy, when he finally managed to get his hands on the plants during an unguarded moment. The wire-and-glass container prevented the saboteur from simply uprooting the little bud, and he only managed to tear off a branch before being caught red-handed.

AROUND JANUARY 20, THE *SS PISA* TOOK A SHARP RIGHT AND headed into the center of the Atlantic Ocean. The flocks of seagulls that had been following us disappeared, and for the next six days we saw almost no living thing. I spent most of my time in the prow reading *Moby Dick* and listening to the sea crash against our hull. Aye, I'm an adventurer just like Ahab, I'd think. Tonight I *will* eat the veal!

Most of the passengers hung around the minuscule swimming pool near the engines. Only Christian and his three-year-old, Luanna, ventured forward on the chance they might see a whale. They saw only a hammerhead shark. We all saw flying fish. There were only twenty people on the SS *Pisa* and I often went half a day without seeing anyone on deck. Three days out, a lone seagull hung about the vessel. We all thought an island was near. But there was nothing. Stars filled the sky every night to overflowing. My tablemates, Sergio and Franco, had a fight and stopped speaking to one another. I began skipping dinner to watch the sunsets. Most were unmemorable, if you exclude the fact that they were uniquely mine—with everyone else inside, and no other humans for thousands of miles, I was the only person who saw at least five of the world's sunsets that January.

On the morning of the twenty-sixth we woke to find seagulls dive-bombing into the sea and coming up with flying fish writhing in their beaks. The lush green island of Pendeos de São appeared on our bow. We were crossing the equator. Captain Vitello summoned the passengers up to the pool, where we were given diplomas for having "graduated" the equator. Then the first mate, dressed as Neptune, baptized the passengers by painting us with melted chocolate and tossing us into the pool.

"Strange graduation ceremony," I said to Christian afterward.

"I am Swiss. We like anything with chocolate." He gave Luanna a squeeze. "You like chocolate too, eh, Luanna?"

"I'm surprised Luanna didn't insist on being thrown into the pool."

I watched the pool, now dark brown from the chocolate, being drained. Luanna began to wail.

"I hope they fill it again soon," said Christian, as the last drop gurgled away. "Luanna will miss her swims."

DE CLIEU MAY NOT HAVE HAD A SWIMMING POOL ON THE *Dromedaire*, but he would have related to Luanna's dismay because it was somewhere near here that he suffered his famous water shortage. It happened when the *Dromedaire*, only a few hundred miles from Martinique, had its hull split during a tropical storm. The storm passed, but the breach could not be sealed. The *Dromedaire* began to sink. Anything unnecessary was thrown overboard, including most of the drinking water.

The storm was followed by a dead calm. A week passed. Then two. Still no wind. Tossing out their drinking water began to seem shortsighted; calms like this were known to last up to a month. Everyone was limited to half a cup of water per day, barely enough for one person, and definitely not enough for a teenage plant. So, in one of the noblest sacrifices in the Caffeinated Age, De Clieu shared his water ration with his precious pet.

"I would have died of thirst to keep alive the plant they had given me," De Clieu wrote. "But listen, you know what glory this precious little plant promised me! If I died, then so be it! But I knew coffee held a glorious destiny for me."

The aristocrat's sacrifice drove the over-caffeinated romantics of the eighteenth-century wild. Poems were written about it, all bad, as per this sample by Charles Lamb:

When'er I fragrant coffee drink
I on the generous Frenchman think,

Whose noble perseverance bore
The tree to Martinico's shore....

But soon, alas! His darling pleasure
In watching this, his precious treasure

Is like to fade—for water fails
On board the ship in which he sails....

Even from his own dry parched lips
He spares it for his coffee slips.

Artists painted the scene, and in 1816 a Dutch merchant had

a special coffee set made commemorating De Clieu's "noble sacrifice." There's a botanical garden named after our chevalier in Martinique and even a species of the plant bearing his name, *Coffea declieuxias*. The best tribute that I've read, though, comes from a class of ten-year-olds whom De Clieu's great-great-great-great-great-great-great-grand-daughter, Madame Cotelle, met with a few years ago:

A notre chevalier (To our poppy)
Amateur de café (lover of coffee)

Allant en Martinique (Went to Martinique)
pres de l'Amerique (near to Amerique)

Sur un grand bateau (On a big boat)
il sacrifia son eau (he sacrificed his water)

Gabriel De Clieu (Mr. De Clieu)
leur fit dises adieux (we bid you adieu)

I may mock, but De Clieu took a serious risk. People completely deprived of water die within four days. Moreover, damage from consuming less than normal amounts of water is cumulative, and his ration was considerably less than half the eight ounces required. His body would at first have compensated by using liquid stored in his cells. This would lead to kidney failure, and as toxins built up in his blood, he would begin to experience stiffness, light-headedness, and eventually hallucinations and death.

None of this happened to Gabriel. The wind picked up, and on an unknown day in an unknown month of a doubtful year, his sole surviving plant reached the island of Martinique. It was the size of a pinky. De Clieu planted it in his garden and put a twenty-four-hour guard on it. Within five years there were over two thousand plants growing on the island. Within fifty years there were eighteen million, and their descendants now supply over 90 percent of the world's coffee.

De Clieu himself proved less fruitful. Although he married four times, only one of his half-dozen children survived, and he eventually passed away in France, landed but poor. Since he was an aristocrat, his tomb at St. Suplice was defiled by the *sans-culottes* of the French Revolution. You can view his anonymous remains today for a mere fifteen francs at the Paris Catacombs, where they lie mingled with countless others.

The *SS Pisa* refilled its swimming pool, and Luanna learned to do the dog paddle. Five days later the faint smell of sulfur told us that we'd arrived in Rio de Janeiro.

Africa in Chains

I prefer to see my mother rot
than sign a letter of liberty for my slaves.

Monito Campert, Brazilian coffee baron, 1888

SLAVERY AND COFFEE HAVE gone hand in hand since enslaved Oromo warriors brought the bean to Harrar. The bitterest irony of this relationship, however, must have been when Africans arrived in the New World and found themselves enslaved in the harvesting of a plant stolen from Africa just as they themselves had been. South American coffee plantations created a demand for slave labor that forever altered both Africa and the New World. Ten years after De Clieu brought his plants to Martinique, the French government began importing thirty thousand slaves a year with the goal of becoming the world's leading coffee supplier. Half the captives died in the attempt, but France succeeded, until 1791, when the slaves of Haiti overthrew their oppressors and became the first free black nation in the Western Hemisphere.

For sheer quantity of slaves, though, Brazil takes the cake. Over a two-hundred-year period, about three million Africans were brought here to work in private coffee kingdoms. An additional five million were enslaved on sugar plantations. By comparison, only half a million total were brought to North America.

This plantation/slave social model remains the basis for modern Brazilian society. Ten percent of the people own 54 percent of the wealth. Direct slave descendants are ten times more likely to be illiterate or destitute. Although half of the citizens are from mixed marriages, most of the children sleeping in the gutter are noticeably dark, while the nubile things frolicking on the beach evince a lighter hue.

"Oh, this is true," said Mario. "But still everybody is friends."

We were sitting on Rio de Janeiro's famous Copacabana beaches watching a game of volleyball. The players were typical Rioites—perfect physiques, skin the color of burnt butter—and although I couldn't tell, Mario, a pale-skinned Brazilian, said that one of the players was pure African.

"You see, he is African, but who cares?" He pointed to a man in red Speedo briefs. "He might even be from the *favela*, a Speedo costs nothing, but it does not matter. The right to play volleyball is in our constitution."

Favelas are hillside shantytowns that occasionally slide off onto the high-rise condos that line Copacabana's beaches. Think Miami with Calcutta on top. Bikinis and leprosy.

"So you're saying because this one guy is playing volleyball, there are no racial problems in Brazil?"

"No, no, of course there are problems. Black people are poorer. But for Brazilians, money isn't everything. Look at your country," he continued. "The black people are rich, like Michael Jackson and the General man [Colin Powell]. But still the black and the white people do not get along. That is because in USA, money is everything. Everyone always wants more. In Brazil, it is not money that is everything, and so people can get along. That is the difference."

"Why do they play volleyball with their feet?" I asked. Our team was serving the ball with their feet, rallying and even slamming. The game, called *footvolei*, is an obsession unique to Rio. These guys were even adjusting radio volume knobs with their feet. "Don't they know that the only difference between man and monkey is we use our hands?"

"Everybody in Rio plays like this," he said. "It is the Rio way."

"You too?" He seemed a tad out of shape for this kind of stuff.

"Everyone but me."

I pointed to a dog who kept dropping a coconut into the middle of the court.

"Maybe the dog wants to teach the people to play a game just using their mouths," I said. "That, he would say, is the dog way."

Mario laughed. He thought I was funny. He spoke my language. He must be planning to rob me.

THE GREATEST OF THE EARLY COFFEE EMPIRES WERE IN THE countryside near Rio de Janeiro and São Paulo, where *faziendas* of two, three, four million plants were common. The plantation I wanted to track down had belonged to the notorious Baron Grão-Mogol, a Portuguese nobleman who had epitomized Brazil's schizophrenic slave society, which, as Mario had said, "still let everyone have fun."

The baron's plantation was in the town of Rio Claro. Back then, Rio Claro was on the edge of the known world. Today it is a São Paulo commuter suburb, full of sulky teenagers aping American pop stars. And hot—Brazil was the hottest place I've ever been, averaging about 120 degrees Fahrenheit for most of my stay. Since my map of the area was a century old, my first stop was City Hall, where I hoped they might have something more up to date. There was a huge line outside the building, apparently for some kind of Lotto game. I asked a man where the planning department was.

"No planning department in this town!" he said. "Nobody plans anything here, I can tell you. There's no plan in all of Brazil."

I found the office and gave a lady named Linda a lie about how I was a student making a list of historical coffee plantations. I asked if she knew the farm belonging to Baron Grão-Mogol.

"Grão-Mogol? Yes, that's Fazienda Angelique. The Rossi family."

"Who are they?" I asked.

"I think they live on the *fazienda* today." She yelled out an order in Portuguese. "Someone is getting the map."

There was a growing babble of voices coming from behind the counter. Apparently half the Rio Claro planning department was on the quest. I asked if the baron had any relatives left in the area.

"They are all gone," she said. "Here, I will show you."

The baron's plantation, it seemed, still existed about seventeen kilometers down a mud road from a village called Ajapi. There were only three buses a day to the village, about twenty miles out of Rio Claro, and she suggested I catch the one at seven A.M. to avoid the heat.

"Thank you," I said. "You've been very kind."

"Of course," said Linda. "If they still grow coffee, please

come back and tell us. We're supposed to be keeping track of these things."

Ajapi turned out to be a single street, glowing white in the morning heat. My ride (I'd hitched when the bus never arrived) let me off in front of an open air café/bar/general store manned by a plump woman with glasses. I went up to the counter and asked for the Brazilian version of espresso, called *cafézinho*. The brew is made by pouring hot water through a sock-like bag containing ground coffee. You then take the resulting liquid and pour it again through the coffee grounds up to ten times, until you achieve the desired strength. The result is a refreshingly bitter brew—the French call it *jus de chausette* ("shoe juice")—which the lady's son, a twelve-year-old boy in a baseball cap, dribbled into a thick-handled demitasse half full of sugar.[1]

I asked the lady, Regina, if she'd ever heard of the baron.

"Oi," she said. "His old farm is maybe five kilometers from here."

"No, no," interrupted her son. "It's seven, maybe eight."

I asked Regina the name of the family that lived there.

"Rossi, of course," she said. "Everyone in Ajapi is a Rossi."

According to Regina, there were about five hundred Rossis in the area. Her café doubled as a communal living room and town hall. There was an outdoor *bocha* (bowling alley) next door with a grill for steaks. On a fine evening you could take your *cerveja* on the faded turquoise bench outside, which also doubled as the village bus station.

"Must be hard having only relatives for customers," I said. "Aren't they always wanting discounts?"

---

[1] This area specializes in an unbearably bitter coffee bean called Riote. Reputedly the world's worst bean, because of its high iodine and salt content, it is a delicacy in New Orleans and Turkey.

She laughed. "Discounts? They're lucky I don't charge them double."

The Rossis had come to Brazil in the mid-1800s during the coffee barons' brief attempt to replace slavery with indentured servants from Europe. The Europeans, however, proved unsuitable. They refused to work the slaves' fourteen-hour days. They built schools. Some even had the gall to be better educated than the barons, most of whom signed their name with an X. To top it off, once they'd paid off their debt, these spoiled Eurotrash had the gall to demand their freedom! The barons immediately returned to the civilized comforts of slavery, and most of the *colonos* headed back to Europe. Of those who remained, only one in ten managed to save enough to buy land.

"I think Pedro Rossi bought a hundred hectares," said Regina. "That was when he bought the baron's old house. Maybe 1920."

She led me to a red mud road and gave me some directions. I asked her a question about the baron's "insane" wife. She gave me a lengthy response. I can understand some Portuguese because I speak Spanish, but with Regina's Paulista accent, it was almost impossible.

"I'm sorry, " I said. "But I didn't understand your answer."

Regina nodded contentedly. "That's okay, I really didn't understand your question."

BARON GRÃO-MOGOL PROBABLY CHOSE THIS AREA FOR HIS plantation because dark red earth was thought to be the ideal coffee-growing environment. The best was called *terra roxa*, "purple earth." The countryside reminded me of an England on steroids. From a distance it looked like manicured green lawns and shrubbery. What I took to be grass, however, turned out to be six-foot-tall palm-like leaves of *soja*. My "hedges" turned out to be towering avocado trees. Everything was such a bright shade of green it hurt my eyes. Poodle-size rodents scurried across the road. A horseman leading a mule appeared in the distance. I stepped into a bit of shade to consider the possibilities.

Kilometers and kilograms have always confused me. I know one is two times its American equivalent and the other is half. Only I just can never recall which is which. Regina had said the plantation was seven kilometers away. So I had either three miles to walk or fourteen, a considerable difference considering that the temperature was well over a hundred. Hence my interest in the approaching mule. There was also an historic angle. Until 1913, donkeys like this were the only transport out of Rio Claro. Tens of thousands of the beasts made the ten-day pilgrimage to the coffee port of Santos. Hundreds died in the pools of quicksand that formed in the rainy season. Others were killed by robbers. Many had their backs broken by their three-hundred-pound loads. Regular coffee martyrs, really, and I thought it would be a fitting tribute to these unsung heroes if I were to arrive at the baron's plantation atop one of their descendants.

Man and mule finally reached me. I asked the man, who was dressed all in white, if he knew the Rossis. He did. I told him I was going for a visit.

"What a beautiful animal," I said, pointing to his mule. "May I pet him?"

He raised an eyebrow. "Of course."

"How far is it to the Rossi farm?" I asked, stroking the mule's flank.

He told me. I expressed my surprise at the distance. I indicated how hot it was. I suggested I had a bad leg. I offered him ten dollars for a ride on his mule.

As we rode along, my friend ran me through the old who-what-where-why, much as if he were one of the baron's soldiers who had roamed the area seeking runaway slaves. The man, who spoke some Spanish, was not a Rossi. But he had heard of the baron. Did I know, he said, that the baron pretended his wife was insane and kept her locked in the attic for twenty years? That he'd fathered hundreds of illegitimate children with his slaves? Had I heard about the sadistic orgies in the basement? The child slave harems?

I had. But the baron was more than a mere *garanhoes fogosos de negralhada* (fiery stallion of the Negress gang). He was also one of the more progressive slave owners and included fifteen of his illegitimate mulatto children in his will. He also made a point of "freeing" his slaves' wombs. This noble declaration, which made children born to slave parents free at birth, came ten years after the government had freed all child slaves, however. The baron's hypocrisy was still pretty minor compared to the nation's largest slaver, who surprised everybody by "confessing" he'd been a closet abolitionist for the last twenty years. His hundreds of slaves, he explained, actually belonged to his wife; he had been merely "managing her estate."

Mules may be fine for carrying coffee beans, but they are less good for transporting Stewarts. Aside from being ridiculously slow, the animal's razor-sharp spine, combined with the gentle sawing motion, would, I felt, soon precipitate a mitosis. I persisted, however, and we soon came to a crumbling mansion on a hilltop.

"That's where the baron lived," he said. "You know, of course, that it is haunted?"

I think I had expected a structure like Rimbaud's house in Ethiopia. The baron's estate was crude by comparison, more fortress than home. Fifteen-foot-high windows, all closed with massive shutters, adorned the second story. The only way to enter the house was via a narrow stone staircase at the side of the building, an arrangement meant to optimize defense in case of a slave rebellion.

After a few moments of calling out from the gate, I entered the yard. What was the etiquette for this, I wondered? To one side of the mansion was a single-story modern house ringed with shrubs. There was also what I took to be a red clay tennis court, but was actually the traditional *terreiro* used to dry coffee beans. I saw a woman watching me from the eaves of the modern house. I waved hello, and she was instantly replaced by a teenage girl in shorts who introduced herself as Carolanne, the great-great-granddaughter of Pedro Rossi, who had bought the place from the baron's descendants in the early 1900s. I told her I was a history student, and she took me inside the mansion.

Up close the house seemed shoddy. The walls were thin and,where the plaster had cracked, I could see they were made of nothing but mud and termite-riddled two-by-fours. The floor shivered underfoot. Shafts of sunlight spilled in through gaps in the red-tiled roof.

"It gets very wet in here when it rains," said Carolanne. Until twenty years ago the Rossis had lived in the mansion. Only workers used it now.

The living room, about seven hundred square feet, contained a gargantuan, worm-eaten oak table that dated back to the baron's time. The only other piece of furniture was a sixties-style, blue-glitter, Naugahyde lounge chair. Most rooms were empty. Carolanne took me upstairs to a claustrophobic attic room. This, she said, was where the baron kept his wife locked up. The sole window looked over the square where slave mothers whose children had died were required to apologize to the baron for not "taking care of his property." It was also where the baron would lead his slaves in prayer.

"Look." Carolanne opened a midget door that led only to a thirty-foot drop. Below were the baron's sleeping quarters, now boarded up. She didn't know why the door had been built. I asked Carolanne if she knew about the baron's torturing of the slaves.

"Of course," she said cheerfully. "Down in the basement."

The basement was full of shattered glass, over which Carolanne walked barefoot.

"Here," she said. "He tied the slaves here."

The baron had used the central support for his home as his whipping post, a thick log sheathed in a heavy black metal casing. The roof, forty feet overhead, seemed to sag away on all sides from where the post touched it, as if it alone kept the house's center from collapsing.

The baron's henchman had been a freed African from northern Brazil who had lived with the Rossis after the baron departed. According to him, Grão-Mogol's soirées were gastronomic, sexual, and sadistic orgies. First there would be a banquet. Then the guests, presumably all male, would descend to the basement to enjoy the favors of whichever female slaves the African freeman had captured and chained below. The baron was president of Rio Claro's county council at the time, so one can be sure that society's finest lights were on hand for the festivities.

I was much too delicate to ask Carolanne if she knew what kind of pain most pleased the baron. We know only that the preferred instrument of torture among the coffee barons was a five-pronged, metal-tipped whip, called the *chicote*. Up to four hundred lashes was not uncommon. Slaves were often whipped to death, a criminal act, so their deaths were reported as a "fulminating apoplexy." Those that survived had salt and vinegar rubbed into their open wounds. Many developed *banzo*, or longing for Mother Africa, which culminated in a slow suicide. Mothers often killed their own babies.

Three feet up the post hung a black iron ring where "he tied them up," according to Carolanne. What a perverse world we live in, I thought, fingering the ring. The baron eventually made his slaves build a monument to him, as "thanks" for their freedom. It still stands. I did not visit. A more fitting monument is the town bearing the baron's name, Grão-Mogol in Minas Gerais. It is the center of the recent rebirth of Brazilian slavery. Peasants are lured to Grão-Mogol with promises of high salaries, only to find themselves living in quasi-prisons and forced to work in coal mines for wages that ensure they will never get out of debt. Those who try to escape are beaten to death. Thanks to places like Grão-Mogol, Brazil now enjoys the highest slavery rate in the Western world, jumping from 597 cases in 1989 to 25,000 in 1996.

I felt something brush against my shoulder. It was Carolanne.

"Are you finished, señor?" she asked. "I need to go do my homework."

SLAVERY WAS NOT THE ONLY THING COFFEE BROUGHT TO THE NEW world, because the Africans brought gods like Ogun, Oxumare, Exu, and, if my guess was correct, the coffee-loving Zar spirits of Ethiopia. This may seem unlikely at first glance. Brazilian slaves were from West Africa, while Zar is strictly East Coast. But hundreds of years before the slavers showed up, Sufi mystics had traveled across northern Africa and, in the course of spreading Islam, they'd seemingly carried the seeds of the Zar cults all the way to Nigeria. While the Nigerian religion, called Bori-Zar, could have existed prior to the Sufis' arrival, the similar-sounding names, along with identical use of dance and trance, indicate a connection.

Nigeria, however, was where the Zar trail seemed to end. I'd consulted dozens of books in London and Paris, but despite the millions of Africans shipped to Brazil, and despite the abundance of Afro-Brazilian religions, there was no direct indication that the Zar cults existed in the New World. This seemed so absolutely illogical to me—I mean, wouldn't the Zar spirits have recognized their beloved bean growing all about them and demanded a cup now and then? So after visiting the baron's house I headed for a place called Valley of the Dawn, which I'd been told was a university dedicated to studying the connections among all the world's religions. There, if anywhere, I was told, I would find my answer.

My informant on all this was a New Age American I'd met in Rio. He told me the valley was near the city of Brasilia.

"It is right in the center." He gave me a knowing look. "Between the fifteenth and sixteenth parallels."

Brasilia, the national capital, was one of the utopian megaprojects of the 1960s, a completely preplanned city constructed in three years in the middle of the Amazonian jungle. Enormous slum-shantytowns surround the city and everyone said it was positively hellish. I didn't find it so bad once I got there—just another empty, ugly city in the middle of nowhere. It reminded me a bit of Los Angeles.

I ended up being guided to the university, set about eighty miles out of Brasilia proper, by a man who attached himself to me while I was waiting for the bus.

"You are going to the Valley?" Before I could respond he'd placed his hand reassuringly on my shoulder. "I'll take you there. We will be friends. My name is Meister."

"Thanks," I said. Meister seemed an odd creature. His sole facial expression was a twitch that writhed across his lips every time our eyes met. It was, I believe, a smile. My new friend sat next to me on the bus. After an hour of curiously bland countryside—Brazil overall reminded me of a golf course—the bus stopped in front of a large yellow arch painted with moons and stars.

"You understand that this is a place of the highest spiritual level possible," he said, pulling me off the bus. "You wish to go in? You wish to see our work?"

"Oh, well, yes," I replied uncertainly. I couldn't stop ogling the crowd on the other side of the arch. This was a university?

"Come!"

He led me through the crowd and into a windowless building. What interesting uniforms everybody was wearing! As my eyes adjusted to the building's light I saw that I was in a long, low room whose walls were covered in symbols from a number of major religions, stars of David, crosses, etcetera, all painted primary red and yellow. At one end of the room sat a twelve-foot statue of an Indian woman holding an enormous steel spear.

"This is where we do our work," Meister said. He led me to a bench. "Wait."

All the women were wearing gauze blouses and skirts made of bunched-up pink and turquoise scarves. The costume seemed vaguely Arabic, especially the headpiece. Actually, they looked like Barbara Eden in the TV sitcom *I Dream of Jeannie*. The men wore skin tight black jeans and ten gallon cowboy hats, with supershort vests ending just below the armpits. I recognized the outfit from another TV show, *Wild Wild West*. A few men wore ankle-length gray capes with six-inch-high collars: Barnabas Collins, of course. What the hell, I wondered, was going on? Everybody was lined up around the Indian statue, palms turned upward, apparently soaking in its mystical vibrations. Two teenage girls sat motionless on either side of the statue.

Meister returned and handed me a cup full of a milky liquid. "Water," he said to my dubious look. "Drink. It cleanses."

I obeyed and pointed to a photograph of a wild-looking

white woman. "Who's that?" I asked.

"That's Tia Neiva," he said, upturning his palms toward the portrait. "Leader."

"Oh," I groaned, politely mimicking the gesture. I knew the name Tia Neiva. She was a woman who had started receiving messages from extraterrestrials while working as a truck driver during Brasilia's construction in the sixties. This wasn't a university. (Obviously, right?) It was a church that had been set up according to instructions sent by a fleet of flying saucers that remained hidden on the other side of the moon. The church's duty, according to Tia's writings, was to prepare the Earth for their landing on December 31, 1999. Every day, hundreds of the priests gather about a huge Star of David floating in a nearby lake (the star is a cosmic radio antenna) to receive messages and recite the following prayer to the people of the planet Capela: "Oh, Simromba of the Great East of Oxala, in the enchanted World of the Himalayas, prepare my way, illuminate my spirit, so that I may go forth fearless in the final advance of the New Age."

I wanted to go home. The combination of the room's heat and the faint smell of vomit was making me feel dizzy. Every time I stood up, however, Meister pushed me back into my seat. "What, you don't want to see our work?" he kept saying, growing increasingly aggressive as the hours wore away. He made me drink some more "water." I noticed that people across the hall were vomiting into buckets. The stench grew thicker. Someone started making a horrible choking, screaming sound.

I brushed aside Meister's hand and left. He followed, urging me to go back so "I would understand." I found the bus and got on, only to realize it was going in the wrong direction. For the next forty-five minutes I rode through dozens of dusty villages, all populated by cult members dressed in those ludicrous outfits. There seemed to be thousands (actually, there are an estimated twenty thousand followers). I rode along with my mouth open in disbelief; I'd had no idea that anything like this existed anywhere. What will these people do, I wondered, when A.D. 2000 rolls past and nothing changes?

Prêto Vêlho

Macaco veio, macaco veio
cafésaja
come que?

Monkey came and the coffee bushes died.
What do we eat now?
Brazilian slave song, circa 1800

I TOOK A BUS HEADED TOWARD Bolivia. My visit to the Valley of the Dawn had left me feeling as if my trip had been cursed, and I decided to give up my search for the Zar cults. It was obvious the Zar spirits did not want to communicate with me.

I was now traveling by day through hundreds of miles of flat green *soja* fields. *Soja* is a palm-like six foot leaf from which oil is extracted. (I felt like an ant in the middle of a football field.) *Soja* is the last step in the Brazilian agricultural cycle, which consists of first burning off the jungle and planting a cash crop like coffee. When this has depleted the soil, you let it rest for a bit and then plant another cash crop, like *coffee*. Everyone knows that the burning of the Brazilian jungle has had a devastating impact on the globe's ecosystem. What most java junkies don't realize is that keeping them supplied has caused a significant part of this havoc. In the past, most South American plantations used "shade" farming, a technique that allows the coffee trees to grow interspersed with traditional foliage. In the mid-1970s, Brazil's plantations switched to the so-called sun growth method. This means that the forest is burned off and only the coffee trees remain.

For workers it means searing sun and heat. For the environment it spells deforestation, greater use of pesticides, and degraded soil quality. The most pressing issue is decreased biodiversity in trees and bird life. Sixty percent of North American birds winter in South and Central America. As the traditional shade plantations disappear, these birds simply have no place to go. Sun plantations support 90 percent fewer bird species than shade farming, according to the Smithsonian Migratory Bird Center in Washington, D.C.

Of late there's been a trend to sell so called shade coffee. This means the beans were grown under the older, more environmentally friendly conditions. There's no quality difference, and it's probably the least any junkie can do to rationalize his or her habit.

After thirty hours of this hell I arrived in the town of Campo Grande near the border. This is cowboy country, and the bus station was designed so that a visiting gaucho could fulfill every need without ever leaving the terminal. There were two porn theaters (*Friday Nite Delite!* was playing during my visit), three barber shops, and bars galore. The stores featured one-stop

"Gaucho Day Care Packs" containing three bags of rice, four bags of beans, Spam, laundry detergent, hair gel, and five bars of soap.

Beyond the bus station was a medium-size town full of leather goods and Spanish one-stories. It's so hot people put their Popsicles in a tumbler between licks and then drink the liquid.

The citizens, oddly enough, are proud of their mild climate.

"You were in Cuiaba?" scoffed the manager of Hotel Continental. "It was 45 degrees Celsius [115 Fahrenheit] there today—here it was only 39 [105]!"

He kicked some kernels of popcorn out of my room.

"I don't understand why this room is so dirty," he said, scowling from under his white fedora. "We are usually very careful about this!"

A few minutes later he returned with an explanation.

"This room still has someone sleeping in it!" he said triumphantly. "I knew there had to be a reason."

He led me to another equally disheveled room. I asked him about the crowd of people I'd seen in front of a nearby building.

"That is the Spiritual Center."

"What is the Spiritual Center?"

"Brazilian spirits."

It was the first lucky break I'd had in Brazil. I had been making inquires about Afro-Brazilian cults in every city I visited, but it's still a secretive movement, since it had only recently been made legal.

The center was my first stop next morning. As I headed out, however, the man at the hotel's front desk stopped me.

"You are the man with the questions for the spirits?" he asked with a big wink. "Questions, eh?"

His name was Mario, a plump fellow with a happy face and

an ear covered in purple mold. He told me that the Spiritual Center was devoted to Kardecism, a quasi-syncretic cult made popular in the 1800s by the French mystic Allan Kardec. Waste of time.

I asked him if he knew of a Candomble temple.

"You want to talk to a Boreesha, eh?" Or that's what I thought he said. It gave me a start: it sounded like he had said Bori-Zar.

"What did you say?"

"Boreesha," he repeated, writing it out on a piece of paper: O-r-i-x-a. I knew the word. Orixas are the spirits of the Afro-Brazilian cults, and I'd seen it a zillion times while doing research in Paris. What I hadn't known was that, spoken, it opens with a muted *b*, and the *x* is pronounced "za." The Candomble Orixas were the Bori-Zar spirits of Africa.

Mario didn't know any Candomble groups. His sister, however, was a priestess of the related Umbanda cult. Would I like to meet her?

"You have questions?" He gave me another of his special winks. "Ah, I know you do."

"Many. How much will it cost?"

Mario raised his hands in horror. "No, no money. There is no need to give money."

"Really?" I liked that. Then I remembered the "present" of green coffee beans I had given the Ethiopian Zar priest. "Should I bring presents?"

"Presents are fine," he said. "They like tequila."

I'D EXPECTED THAT IF THE ZAR RELIGION EXISTED HERE IT WOULD be part of the popular Candomble religion. But it appeared to be more prominent in the Umbanda group, an Candomble offshoot popular among Brazil's poorer urban population. Candomble predominates in the north, the traditional center for

African culture, whereas Umbanda is more popular in the south. Both groups worship at churches called *terreiros*, named after the clay courts used to dry coffee beans like the one I'd seen at Baron Grão-Mogol's home. Both call their spirits Orixas, a name derived from the Bori-Zar cosmology. Candomble's Orixa sprits, however, retain traces from the days when African slaves disguised their gods as Catholic saints. The pantheon includes hermaphroditic Oxamare, who likes champagne, and Oxala, who prefers offerings of white corn. Umbanda Orixas, for reasons I don't understand, are much closer to the Ethiopian Zar spirits inasmuch as they are based on racial archetypes like *o caboclo*, an American Indian spirit, and the European warrior, *o guerreiro*. The most powerful spirit, though, is Preto Velho, the spirit of the old African slave, whose favorite offering is, of course, coffee, fresh-roasted just like it was when he was growing up in Africa two thousand years ago.

When Mario's friend, Walter, appeared to drive me to the Umbandan priestess the next day, I had a pound of coffee beans handy, as well as a box of cigars and a bottle of rum. Walter, a puffy-looking white man with sad eyes, eyed the rum.

"I'm divorced," he said, apropos of nothing.

The priestess was still asleep when we arrived at her shack. Walter and I waited in her clay courtyard. Over the fence I could see Campo Grande's modern downtown skyline. Sitting in a witch doctor's courtyard and seeing a twentieth-century skyline seemed terribly Brazilian; the country seems to exist half in a Frank Lloyd Wright/bikini daydream and half in a traditional African village.

A bald turkey wandered up and gave me the evil eye. A boy offered us water. The priestess, Neva, wandered out and launched into a lecture about Preto Velho.

"Preto Velho is very serious," she said. "He doesn't like bad things. He thinks very deeply about all. You don't fool with him, because he has suffered so much. Around his ankles are the scars from the chains used to enslave him, and his wrists too. His back is covered with scars from the master's whipping, and sometimes you have to bring his coffee to his lips because he's still hanging by his wrists in the slave boats. He's old, old and wise, Father Africa, which is why he comes when he smells the coffee being roasted, because coffee came from where he was born. But as much as coffee, he likes his pipe. Nothing makes him happier than to sit in his chair of an evening with his pipe and a glass of wine."

Preto Velho, she said, loves the little children. There is a special holiday for them in September, "when all the little ones they come and they visit with him. It makes him very happy."

If I'd seen Neva on the street I would have thought she was a secretary. She was a broad-shouldered woman with a square face, a look accented by her close-cropped afro. She dressed like an aerobics instructor: pink tights and a tacky white sweatshirt. Her lips were painted bright red. She told me about the other African spirits, particularly Escrava Anatasia, a woman with a cruel iron muzzle over her mouth "so she cannot scream all the pain she has suffered at the hands of her slave owners." I thought about the Baron Grão-Mogol's sadistic orgies.

"You have seen Preto, no?" she asked. I had seen many statues. He is portrayed as a kindly African grandfather dressed in white, wearing a wide-brimmed straw hat. He's usually seen relaxing in a chair with a corncob pipe in his hand.

"Ahh, yes, he loves the pipe. Not so much cigars." She waved to the box I had brought. "He likes his pipe and his wine and his coffee. These are the good things. And so—you would like to speak to Preto Velho, yes?"

I hesitated. After all, I wasn't really a believer. I thought it would be disrespectful to put her through the ordeal of being possessed. But I did want to speak to him; of course I did.

Neva saw the truth.

"Come," she said. "I see you do."

She led Walter and me back to a room with the sign TENDA OGUN hanging over the door. There were lit candles and, at one end, a long table covered with Umbandan statues. There were about a dozen versions of Preto Velho and a variety of Catholic saints including St. George and the Virgin Mary. There was a statuette of an Indian woman I recognized from the Valley of the Dawn. One that I found particularly puzzling was a blue-eyed blond girl sucking her pinky.

"Here," Neva was excited, like a child about to play with a favorite uncle. She thrust a simple pipe into my hands. "This is Preto Velho's pipe—I told you how he loves it. Oh, how he loves that pipe! He does!"

She had Walter fill it with tobacco. She made me strike a tom tom. "This is to wake him. He's always napping, that one!" she said, laughing. "But this will wake the lazy old one!" She began beating out a simple one-two rhythm, chanting "Ti-a Mar-ia! Ti-a Maria!" to a bleak little tune. I noticed a three-foot Preto Velho figure on the table. He seemed to be leaning forward on his cane.

"This is his cane!" Neva shouted in my ear. She shoved a white cane into my hand. Its handle was carved into the likeness of an African man. "He's so old! So old! That's why he needs that cane. Better not call him if you don't have a cane for him to lean on!" She was crossing herself, kissing the tablecloth, banging on the drum, and chanting simultaneously. A friend wandered into the room, her hair in pink curlers, and lit the pipe. Neva was consumed in a convulsive shiver, and Preto Velho was with us.

He was an old fellow, bent double with age, stumbling about

the room and muttering to himself. Someone grabbed the cane out of my hands and gave it to him. Someone else pulled up a stool. Preto sat and immediately started complaining in a broken voice—where was his pipe? he wanted to know. Walter handed it to him, and for a few minutes Preto sat mumbling and smoking. I noticed how the whitewashed walls glowed in the light. Finally, Preto took Walter's hands and gave him a quick blessing. Then it was my turn.

I asked a few token questions about money, the future. But my real question concerned my girlfriend, Nina. I had been unable to reach Nina at the number she'd given me, and after our tumultuous parting in India, I wasn't sure she wanted to have anything to do with me. I asked Preto whether I should return to her in New York or head back to my brother's house in California.

One of the most infuriating things about speaking Spanish in Brazil was that they understood me but I often couldn't understand them. Preto Velho comprehended my question and answered it at length. But his Portuguese, two hundred years old and with bits of some African dialect thrown in, was completely incomprehensible. The only thing I was sure I understood was when he demanded to know if I had understood him. I always replied yes; I just couldn't bring myself to ask a thousand-year-old African spirit to try speaking a little slower.

As Preto Velho answered my questions, I studied Neva's face. It had crumbled in half. Her eyes seemed to have disappeared into two wrinkled puckers of darkness. The voice was still hers, but now shivered with age. Spittle drooped from her lips, and her breath reeked of tobacco, the smell seeming to come from every pore in her body, as if she'd been smoking that pipe for centuries. It was utterly convincing, and while I'm not quite sure I was speaking with the archetypal spirit of all enslaved Africans, I'm not sure I wasn't; I'm absolutely certain Neva thought I was.

While Preto spoke with me, Walter and the lady in the hair curlers chatted about the weather. This bit of mundane behavior made the whole situation more plausible. The lady in curlers finally asked if I had any more questions. I said no. Preto blessed first me and then the lady. There was a quick shiver, Preto Velho was gone, and Neva was chattering excitedly about an upcoming fiesta. It's so hot in here, she said, why don't we go out in the yard?

"So," Neva asked as we were leaving. "Did Preto Velho speak with you?"

"Yes," I said. "Thank you."

On the drive back, Walter and I were both silent. It had been his first visit, and although he was a Catholic, he'd been impressed. She was, we both agreed, "*muy formidable*." I asked if he wanted five or ten dollars for the gas. He wanted fifteen. I was a tad disappointed that we had not roasted the coffee beans, as they did in Ethiopia. Neva had said it was not necessary. "What, he has wine and cigars—that's not enough for the old man?" I just thought it would have been nice to share a cup with the old fellow, who, despite all the suffering the bean had caused him and his people, still loved the brew as much as I.

Of course, I still had no idea what future he had foretold for me. I found out that evening, when I bumped into Mario and Walter at the counter. Mario burst out laughing.

"So," he said, with one last lascivious wink. "Your questions are answered! You're going back to New York to marry that girl Nina, eh?"

Officer Hoppe

What do you call a large,
low-fat latté made with decaf espresso?
A tall-skinny-why bother.

Grafitti at the L-Café, Williamsburg, NY

THE UNITED STATES WAS THE first Western nation to be born completely caffeinated. Conceived, even, because Captain John Smith, who founded the Jamestown colony in 1607, had met joe while putzing about the Middle East. The Mayflower that brought over the first pilgrims also contained a mortar and pestle for making "coffee powder." By 1669, coffee laced with cinnamon and honey was being poured in New York. America's first legal coffeehouse opened a year later in Boston under the proprietorship of a woman named Dorothy Johnson.

Like their counterparts in Mother England, America's colonial cafés quickly developed a reputation for brewing bad coffee and big business. Boston's Merchant Coffeehouse was the scene of the first public stock auction, while Wall Street's Tontine Coffeehouse became the New York Stock Exchange. This started to change in the 1700s when Britain began its historic transformation from a society of coffee lovers to one based on tea. It's complicated, but essentially England, despite its enormous colonial territories, had failed to acquire any significant coffee-growing plantations. France held most of the Caribbean, Portugal controlled Brazil, and Indonesia belonged to the Dutch. This meant that every cup of java downed by British subjects put money in the pockets of European competitors. Mind you, Great Britain didn't have any tea-producing colonies either. The only drug production they controlled were the opium farms of northern India, a product useless to the British but coveted by the Chinese, who, as luck would have it, had gargantuan tea plantations. So the Brits began trading Indian opium for Chinese tea.[1] They started with reasonable exchange rates, which, as more and more Chinese got hooked on heroin, they raised. By 1750 they were selling tea to the English for half the price of coffee and with a significantly higher profit margin. The company then launched its insidious "The Cup That Cheers" ad campaign and Europe's first great café society became an historical footnote.

---

[1]This eventually led to the infamous "Opium Wars," in which the British government invaded China to ensure that its population remain addicted to opium; for the first time, one nation of junkies fought another to ensure the security of their "stash." The temporary tea shortage brought on by the war also lead to an ill-fated attempt to commercialize the ancient Ethiopia coffee-leaf beverage *kati*. A Dr. Stenhouse marketed it to Britain's lower classes as an alternative to tea, describing it as "a very tolerable beverage...going for twelve pence a pound." According to the *London Critic*, the experiment failed because "Dr. Stenouse's knowledge of chemistry seems superior to his acquaintance with the habits of mankind or he would have commended tea-coffee (*kati*) to the higher classes and rested assured" that it would spread to the lower classes from there.

We colonials were in the process of making the same switch when King George hit the colonies with a tax on tea. At first Americans boycotted the drink. Then a group of patriots disguised themselves as Indians and pushed a shipload of the stuff into Boston Harbor, precipitating the American Revolution, and ensuring that coffee forever after remained the only cup a red-blooded, gun-loving, TV-addled American would be seen drinking in public. We became a nation of java junkies, wired from dawn to dusk, intent on running faster, getting richer, dancing harder, playing longer and getting higher than anybody else.

Funny that we never learned how to make the stuff.

MY ORIGINAL PLAN, AFTER FLYING FROM BRAZIL TO NEW YORK, had been to drive across the United States in search of the perfect cup of coffee. The deepest, richest, most fragrant drip; the loftiest cappuccino; the pithiest espresso. Caffeinated Kerouac. Quest for the Holy Grail. Whatever.

"That's all wrong, man," Jeff said. "Real American coffee is bad. You should be looking for the worst cup, not the best."

Jeff and I were sitting in Odessa's, a classic coffeeshop in Manhattan's East Village, waiting for Nina. My fears regarding myself and Nina had proved happily imaginary, by the way, and I'd soon wormed my way into her squinch-sized apartment in aren't-we-artsy Williamsburg. Jeff was Nina's friend, a grizzled gentleman, leader of the legendary Lefty Jones Band, and dedicated drinker (not necessarily of coffee). His theory was simple: I should not search for mere technical perfection but rather seek the truest, most soulful, of cups, American soul, which flourishes only in the bottom of a mud stew poured out of a Pyrex coffeepot by a farm-faced waitress in a gingham dress and frilly apron; and poured again and again and again and again and again until the customer runs screaming into the night. How could I disagree? America is celebrated the world over not only for using the foulest of beans, but also for brewing them in the most offensive manner possible. And ironically weak—a true-blue joe is both as watery as the Mississippi River and as plentiful, as illustrated by this anonymous turn-of-the-century tale of how the world's first bottomless cup of coffee came into being.

According to the story a traveler, stopping at a country hotel in Mississippi, astonished the owner by drinking cup after cup of coffee. "You seem to be very fond of coffee," the host could not but remark as he tendered the stranger his fifth cup.

"I am indeed, sir," replied the other gravely. "I always take *one* cup of coffee at breakfast, and I am still in hopes of arriving at that quantity before I leave the table. Will you favor me, sir, with another cup or two of this preparation?"

"Yeah, like that," said Jeff, hearing the tale from me. "That's the kinda cup you gotta find."

Nina J. arrived, friends in tow, and three hours and seven gin-and-tonics later it was decided we would take Jeff's golden Cadillac[2] along the legendary Route 66 in search of the worst cup America had to offer. Five brave souls took vows that night: Jeff and his girlfriend, Chris, Nina J. and Stewart, and Nina's best friend, Meg. They flaked, one by one, until, two weeks later, the two surviving members of the expedition, Meg and Stewart, met to make the journey. Jeff's Caddie had been replaced by a driveaway, a Honda Accord of inscrutable hue, which we had one week to deliver to Los Angeles. We equipped ourselves with an unlimited supply of cassettes and half a dozen versions of the caffeinated experience, including Stimu-Chew (caffeinated gum), Water-Joe and Krank (caffeinated

---

[2] Prophetically enough, the term Golden Cadillac is Alabama prison slang for a cup of coffee with milk and sugar.

water), and various types of caffeinated candy. Our prized possession, though, was a vial of pure, gleaming caffeine. I'd scored it from one of the Internet's myriad caffeine fanatics, Seric, who had a site hung with twitching eyeballs.

Meg and I set off around eight P.M., shooting straight south through New Jersey and Pennsylvania, then alongside the Appalachian Mountains of Virginia and Kentucky through Georgia and on into Tennessee. I drove all night. Dead bugs, white lines, and gas stations from outer space. Meg with her feet on the dashboard. She's a tall girl, maybe six feet, with a head of frizzy red hair, and bulging blue eyes that give the illusion that she finds everything you say fascinating. Meg took the wheel at dawn. My next memory is of stepping out into the little town of Athens, Tennessee, at ten A.M. It was already ninety-four degrees. I looked over at Meg and sneered at her appearance. She returned the favor. Then we staggered into a coffeeshop called the Breakfast Nook.

"Morning, folks," said the waitress. "What'll it be?"

It was a squirt of a joint, just a counter facing a griddle. The menu was a creamy white sign with magnetic letters. There were Belgium waffles, links, eggs over easy, eggs Benedict, blueberry pancakes, and scrambled eggs.

The waitress caught me eyeing the sign.

"Don't you pay any 'tention to that, honey," she said. "That's older than me." She pointed to a grease-smeared card taped next to the griddle. "That's the *real* menu. But all we got today is biscuits 'n' gravy."

"Oh," I said. "What's gravy?"

"Well, gravy is what you pour over things," she explained.

This universal covering proved to be a slurry dotted with droplets of yellow fat and curly meat byproducts. While I struggled through the mire, Meg chatted the waitstaff up. There were two of them, both the same shade of overheated pale, both wearing frayed jean shorts.

"Memphis? Y'all taking 240? That's about twelve hours," they said.

"But it's only two hundred miles. That's slower than the train from Addis Ababa," I said.

"Haven't been over to Addis," said one. "Where you folks from?"

"Manhattan," said Meg. "New York."

"That so? You know, I didn't know they had reds in New York."

"Reds?" Meg asked.

"Well, like you, honey. Do you mind me asking if it's real?"

"My hair?" said Meg. "Yeah, sure. It's really red."

"Well, there *you* said it," she chuckled. "Y'all drive careful now and keep an eye peeled for patrol cars. There's lots of speed traps on that road."

She spoke the truth. No sooner had we crossed Athens' city limits than a Tennessee state trooper forced us to pull into a Kwiki convenience store/gas station. One of our brake lights didn't work, so the officer just had to check our license plates, IDs, car registration, and insurance. We also were subjected to a slew of intrusive and unwarranted questions about our personal lives. His name was Officer Hoppe, and I'm sure the resemblance to Ken Starr was a coincidence. He wanted to know where we were going, how we'd met, and although he didn't actually ask us if we were sleeping together, he clearly had his suspicions.

In the end our papers checked out. He asked me to step back to his patrol car one last time.

"Well," he said regretfully, "everything seems on the up and up." He leaned close and gave me a piercing look. "Now, can you guarantee me that there's nothing illegal in that there vehicle?"

The answer was sad but true. We'd wanted to bring some hashish, but Meg's pending entrance into medical school had made the risk too great. Doctors are only allowed to deal legal drugs.

"Nope, nothing illegal," I said.

"That's good. So you won't mind me searching your vehicle then?"

I immediately thought of the vial of caffeine. Totally legal, but there's no denying that a vial full of white powder might raise some eyebrows.

"Well," I hemmed, "can't say I'm terribly enthusiastic."

"Now, why might that be? You did promise me that there was nothing illegal in the vehicle, didn't you?"

"Indeed I did, officer. And there isn't. But I should warn you that you might find something that looks illegal. Only it's not."

Hoppe gave me a condescending smile. "Don't you worry about that, son," he said. "I know what I'm doing. Now, I need you to sign here giving me permission to search your vehicle."

This was like a burglar asking for a receipt. If I refused, Hoppe would take us down to the station while he tried to get a warrant. At the very least, we'd have to wait around Athens all day. And if some idiot actually give him a warrant, he'd never believe the caffeine was anything less than Burmese heroin.

"You gave him *permission*! Are you crazy?" Meg and I were now locked in the back seat of Hoppe's patrol car. Two other cops had joined our friend and were going through the Honda with a fine-tooth comb. Very thorough, for a bunch of bumpkins. "I would never have given him permission! He has no right."

"He *does* have a gun," I pointed out. "I *am* a coward."

"Great!" said Meg. Hoppe was marching over with a gleeful smile. He had the vial in his right hand.

"Now, didn't y'all promise there was nothing illegal in your vehicle?" he asked after rolling down the window.

"Yes," I said. "Didn't you promise me your back seat was going to be air-conditioned?"

"And what's this?"

"It's one hundred percent caffeine, one hundred percent legal." I mentioned I had bought it through the Internet.

"The Internet?" Obviously a dark and mysterious place in the mind of Officer Hoppe. "I'm afraid I'm going to have to place you under arrest for possession of a suspicious substance."

"If you think it's cocaine, why don't you just taste it?" I said. "Cocaine makes your gums go numb, right?"

Hoppe gave me The Look. Boy, it said, you jes' blew your story.

"I couldn't say if cocaine does that, sir. You two just sit tight. We've asked a federal marshal to come by and take a look."

Another patrol car pulled up while we waited for the feds. Then another. Soon there were half a dozen Tennessee state trooper cars camped out around us, and the officers were strutting about, laughing, and passing our little vial from hand to hand.

"They're creaming their pants," moaned Meg. "They're going to throw a couple of New Yorkers in jail. This must...oh my God."

A dark-blue sedan with tinted windows had roared into the station. An overweight officer, wearing a polyester suit and wraparound sunglasses, jumped out. The feds had arrived.

"Glad to be of service, fellas!" we heard him boom. "What seems to be the problem?"

One of the officers pointed to where we sat giggling in the

car. ("Look, those drug addicts are beginning to go through them withdrawals, I reckon."). Mr. FBI eyed us contemptuously and then held the vial up to the sun. He shook his head in disgust. Another officer, an older man, ran me through the same old questions. He was nice enough, however, to let Meg go get something to drink in the convenience store.

"Caffeine?" he said after I'd explained again. "I'm not even sure if it is legal. If that's what you got in the baggie." He jerked his thumb to where Efrem Zimbalist was fumbling about with his high school chemistry kit. "We'll know pretty soon."

"Oh really?" I said. "Did you read in the newspaper about the guy who had his grandmother's ashes in his car and got searched, just like this, but when they tested the ashes they identified it as cocaine?"

"That so? Now, where do you get that stuff anyway?"

I explained how caffeine extracted from decaffeinated coffee beans supplies the buzz in soft drinks (which, by the way, supply almost 50 percent of the caffeine Americans consume). An average cup of coffee has from one hundred to two hundred milligrams, soda pop about fifty to one hundred. So the ten grams in my vial equaled about one hundred cups of coffee and would probably have killed me if I'd taken it in one go. Pure caffeine like that is concentrated enough that you can take it via tongue absorption, thus avoiding the upset stomach that is the drug's main drawback.

"You put it on your *tongue?*" said the officer. "Now that jes' can't be legal."

Meg bounced up back to the car. She'd spilled a bottle of water on her T-shirt, and the result seemed to put the local officers in a more accommodating frame of mind. Not Efrem, though. He completed his tests, ordered me over to his car, and told me to place my hands on the hood. Meg was told to get back in the patrol vehicle.

"That's right my friend," he said with a smirk. "I'm afraid your toys tested positive. One hundred percent pure cocaine."

"Are you serious?" This was getting out of control. I knew it was caffeine, but if their tests were off... Then again, did I really know what Seric had put in the vial? "It can't be cocaine."

"You don't sound so sure about that." He eyed me with delight. "They say you bought it off the Internet, is that right?"

"Yeah."

"So you don't really know what the hell this stuff is, do you? How much did you say you paid for that, boy?"

"Ten dollars," I said. "It's about ten grams, so if that's cocaine..."

"You got one hell of a deal." He laughed and slapped me on the back. "One *hell* of a deal, boy." He and the other cops had a laugh. Then he got back into his car and roared off.

Hoppe and his gang gathered round.

"Now, look here, we don't know what this stuff is," said Hoppe. "It might be legal and it might not. But we're going to let you go. On one condition. You're going to have to pour it out onto the side of the road there, with all of us watching." He handed me back the vial. "It's for your own good. If they caught you with that in Kentucky, they'd hang you."

"So you mean to say I've got to destroy it even though it's perfectly legal?"

"Now, we don't *know* that for a fact. It *might* be illegal," interrupted Hoppe. "But you've been cooperative, and we're willing to give you the benefit of the doubt."

Well, thank you, Officer! I felt like saying. But, frankly, Athens was becoming old news. So I marched over to the highway and poured the white powder onto the blacktop. I'm surprised they didn't take pictures—Another Victory in the American War

Against Drugs! The cops seemed happy, never mind that they'd violated my civil rights, forced me to destroy perfectly legal property, and generally been schmucks. But courteous. They even gave me a "receipt" for the search.

"You should keep that, it'll be handy when other police search you." What, I thought, you need a receipt to avoid getting searched nowadays? Hoppe shook my hand. "Now, you make sure and get that brake light fixed, hear?

I WAS PLEASED TO SEE THAT HOPPE'S HAM-HANDED SEARCH HAD not damaged my ancient 486 laptop computer, which, with a wireless modem, was my link to the Internet. The Net is the latest manifestation, or equivalent, of the coffeehouse as a social institution, a place where anybody can gather, regardless of social standing, and exchange intelligible opinions. The Net evolved from scientists sending notes to one another to sites divided according to subject, just as London's coffeehouse conversations had become Richard Steele's *Tatler*, which in turn spun off into separate specialized magazines.

It's no coincidence that the oldest image on the Net is of a live coffeepot in a Cambridge computer lab,[3] or that cybercafés, where people can "meet" and chat, number in the thousands. So as Meg and I rolled along the highway we were also cruising the Net, creating what can best be described as a café-on-wheels with over a hundred million customers, to whom I immediately dropped a note about Officer Hoppe.

"That's prohibition for you," wrote proffs@tcsx.net on the

[3] This unprepossessing drip coffeepot was first put online in 1991, years before the World Wide Web existed. It was the only coffeepot the hackers at Cambridge owned and appeared in the corner of the lab's computer screens so that people in remote parts of the lab knew when fresh coffee was being brewed. The Trojan Room pot has now been viewed by hundreds of thousands of people, making it without a doubt the world's most famous pot of coffee. It is best appreciated in cyberspace. The appalling quality of the joe inside is legendary.

alt.psychedelics discussion group. "They are scum shit bags who are driven by their abominable addiction to fucking over people. The good people of this nation, this world, are going to rise up and smite prohibitionists from the face of this earth. They're a plague on freedom, and justice, and there will be no weeping for them when they're gone."

The Net is as full of paranoid babblers as was any eighteenth-century café. Hoppe's antics quickly gave birth to a theory that the government was planning to treat coffee like tobacco. "Next it will be Coca-Cola, then sugar, then water, then air," wrote one. A nurse posted that her supervisor ordered her to "seek counseling" for her caffeine habit. Other late-night nurses reported that they now needed their bosses' clearance before they drank a coffee or Coke. In one hospital, the administration had removed all caffeinated drinks from the vending machine. Double-Jolt Cola, containing over a hundred milligrams of caffeine, is apparently illegal in Australia. One of the alt.coffee discussion group's recent debates was whether or not baristas are morally obliged to ask customers' ages before they pull them a double espresso.

It isn't all Net gossip. The federal Food and Drug Administration now monitors products with caffeine, and drug-testing companies are offering preemployment "caffeine abuse screenings" on Net bulletin boards. The Olympic Games Committee now classifies caffeine with steroids as an illegal doping agent and, in 1993, stripped the European breaststroke champion of her award when she tested positive for drinking the equivalent of six cups of coffee.[4] Within the last five years, a twelve-step group called Caffeine Anonymous was created in Portland,

[4] Tests indicate that drinking two cups of strong coffee enhances athletic performance in 75 percent of the population.

Oregon, to help junkies throw away the coffee crutch.

"We were all standing there twitching in line at a Starbucks," said one Net posting from a group member. "Everyone was saying, 'Come on, let's go, let's go. What's the holdup?' We were like heroin junkies."

A report by the National Institute on Drug Abuse says five thousand Americans are killed by caffeine each year, the same number as die from all illegal drugs combined. By comparison, alcohol kills 125,000 (not including accidents), and marijuana zero. Coffee's status as an addictive substance was recognized by the American Psychiatric Association (APA) in 1994. It now categorizes coffee and other caffeine-containing substances with socially unacceptable drugs like heroin and nicotine. The APA's *Diagnostic Statistical Manual of Mental Disorders* states that "subjects can be intoxicated with the excessive use of caffeine and...subjects can become clinically dependent on caffeine." According to the APA, 94 percent of coffee drinkers suffer "Caffeine Dependence Syndrome," whose symptoms include an uncontrollable temper, vomiting, exhaustion, paranoia, and, apparently, delusions of being a computer modem.

"After the day was over, I'd consumed *so* much coffee...I lay in bed completely convinced I was a modem—this is *no* joke," read a Net posting that flickered onscreen as we cruised through Little Rock, Arkansas. "I was lying in bed, concentrating very hard on taking incoming calls and making sure I gave out all the correct tones. It was like the caffeine had completely twisted my mind."

"Caffeine is a psychoactive drug...so it's not such a far stretch that he thought he was a modem," added mthorog@webtb.net to the above message. "I've had it with people treating caffeine as if it were as harmless as water."

None of this is news to the Pentagon, which has been using coffee to enhance violent behavior since 1832, when President

Andrew Jackson replaced the army ration of rum with coffee (six pounds of coffee for every hundred soldiers). This made Union soldiers in the Civil War the first officially caffeinated warriors since the Ethiopian Oromos, getting wired on a brew resembling "the Missouri River on a bender," according to military documents. Soldiers became so fond of the fuel that while officials occasionally cut the food ration, they doubled the coffee supply. The South, hopelessly decaffeinated by a naval embargo, went down to inglorious defeat.[5]

The Civil War proved that coffee enhanced a soldier's physical performance. But more intriguing to the Pentagon were indications that it possessed powerful psychological uses. "In some cases, extreme delusional states of a grandiose character appear...usually of reckless, unthinking variety," wrote J. D. Crother in a 1902 study. "A prominent general in a noted battle in the Civil War, after drinking several cups of coffee, appeared on the front of the line, exposing himself with great recklessness. He was supposed to be intoxicated. Afterward it was found that he used nothing but coffee." Coffee, it seemed, was a general's dream drug—a few cups, and his troops would be rushing to the front line, regardless of the danger. This impression was supported by later military studies like one on "Caffeine-induced hemorrhagic auto-mutilation," which indicated that caffeine made rats so hyperaggressive that they bit themselves to death.

The army began developing a "militarily practical" coffee sometime in the 1800s, according to *Coffee for the Armed Forces*, a document released by the Office of the U.S. Military,

[5] It seems the Confederates attempted in vain to mitigate the lack of joe by adopting a traditional Native American caffeinated beverage called *dahoon*. Derived from the cassina plant, Native Americans in the South had used it as a drink reserved "for their great men and Captains who have been famous for the great Exploits of War and Noble Actions," according to historian Ralph Holt. At one point a caffeinated wine was made from the plant.

Quartermaster General. There were three requirements: it had to be lightweight, long-lasting, and easy to ingest. The first version was an "extract that came in a dense and solid cake," which Congress authorized for military use in 1862. This was thought to be ideal, because it required no packaging and you did not have to brew it, only "mingle" it with cold water to produce the "psychological effect." In a pinch, a soldier could "brew" it with his own saliva, like chewing tobacco. According to military documents, each half ounce "mixed with the saliva [was] as restorative to the system as half a pint of coffee."

If it sounds horribly familiar, it should. What we're talking about is the world's first instant coffee, a military development which would set back American coffee brewing for decades.[6]

The "coffee chaw" disappeared at the end of the Civil War. The army pressed on and, building on a version used by Captain Baldwin on the Zeigler Arctic Expedition, produced a "militarily successful" powder in 1903. Its first battlefield test came in World War I. Fifteen factories produced six million pounds a month. Military consumption jumped 3,000 percent. By WWII there were 125 field roasting plants and twenty-two domestic plants churning out instant for our boys. The daily ration tripled to two ounces (about six strong cups). Even parachutists carried little packets when they dropped behind enemy lines. These were later replaced with the notorious "358 Magnum" capsules, containing about three hundred milligrams of pure caffeine.[7] After

---

[6] The term *Cup of joe* appears to have military roots also. Admiral Josephus "Joe" Daniels, Chief of Naval Operations, not only outlawed booze on U.S. Navy ships but banned the sale of alcohol to soldiers in uniform (he also ended the practice of handing out free condoms). He made coffee the "official" drink of the U.S. Navy, apparently giving birth to the term *cup of joe* in his honor. There is, however, some dispute on the matter; the other theory is that the nickname is a contraction of *mocha-java* to *mo-jo* to *joe*.

[7] The Air Force kept pace by inundating night pilots with Vitamin A (supposed to improve vision). It also handed out Vitamin B supplements, because it was believed to make people less sensitive to noise, and so, less likely to become shell-shocked.

the war, the Joint Army–Air Force Chiefs of Staff held blind tastings to find the most lethal blend for nonfield use. They deadlocked, and the blends sampled remained classified. In 1999 the government gave the military $250,000 to develop a new and improved type of caffeinated chewing gum.

Unlike the "coffee chaw" of the Civil War, instant coffee did not disappear at the end of WWII. Instead, millions of soldiers and nurses returned with Proustian associations linking the taste of instant with some of their most vivid life experiences. Domestic consumption skyrocketed, and by 1958 one third of America's coffee was instant. The trend continued until the Vietnam War, when veterans tasted only the bitterest of dregs in a mug of Taster's Choice. The stage was set for a coffee renaissance. Coincidentally, two years before the end of the war, Starbucks opened its first café.

White-trash Cocaine

Sleep? Isn't that some inadequate substitute for caffeine?

rave@bleach.deamon.co.uk

By now we were deep in Oklahoma and doing serious research. I won't torture you with descriptions of what we went through: the endless Stuckey's, the Cracker Barrel Coffeehouses, the Pojo's, Hardee's, and Denny's; the faceless chains that have erupted across our nation like pus-filled sores, oozing a joe weak, bitter, and vile. "You're in coffee hell," e-mailed one man, but he could have left out the word *coffee*. We were driving across a plain greasy with heat, broken only by clusters of sagging trailer homes trembling with the vibrations of their ancient air conditioners. Yea, verily, we had come to the Land of the White Trash, where methedrine is the morning pick-me-up of choice. Those of you who take offense at my use of the term white trash, by the by, should be aware that I speak with authority, having a pedigree (on the American side) of three generations of moonshiners, striptease artists, and check forgers from South Carolina.

Meg, being a native Manhattanite, thought it all *trés* romantic. "You know, I sort of like it here," she kept saying. "I think this is real America. I bet these people are just the sweetest things."

"Cupcakes," I said, "every last one of them."

We ended up crashing in a hotel a few miles off the main highway—I have no idea where—called the Western Sands, a one-story, L-shaped motor hotel with a gravel-filled parking lot. As I walked up to the registration office my feet crunched on hundreds of semiconscious locusts.

"Rooms are thirty-three dollars, but it ain't no Holiday Inn," said the man at the desk. He seemed to be in his underwear. He reached beneath his waistband for a hearty scratch. "I'll give it to you for twenty-five."

And I hadn't even asked for a discount. Yet I hesitated, for it was true that the Western Sands lacked a certain panache. The teeny lobby was covered with cigarette butts—on the floor, on the counter, on the couch—scattered about like leaves blown in by an autumnal wind. The carpet, what I could see of it through the Budweiser cans, and crusty-looking milk cartons, was polka-dotted with burn holes.

The receptionist was fumbling through the trash on his desk.

"I'm sorry, I can't find the register. I'm just so tired, I swear. You know, where you get that tired you don't jes' fall asleep, you jes' fall off?"

"Fall off?"

"One hundred percent. Gone. But I can't, you know?"

"Can't what?" I asked.

"Fall off, of course."

"Right." He seemed to be getting excited. "Maybe if you just drank some coffee," I suggested.

"Oh, I don't drink that stuff. My stomach's mighty sensitive these days." He gave me a conspiratorial grin. "Just milk and cornflakes, y'know."

His teeth were the color of varnished wood. Speed addict, I thought. White-Trash cocaine. That explained his fondness for cornflakes and milk (to settle the stomach) and his disjointed speech.

"Here it is! I can give you Room 18." His eyebrows raised in surprise. "I think it's been cleaned not too long ago."

"Hi there! What are you boys up to?" It was Meg. She cast a quick glance around the room, and her eyes bugged out a bit more than visual. Fortunately, she'd traveled in Asia and took the Western Sands in stride. "You got a room for us?"

"Sure do," muttered the man. "Long as you're not expecting nothing special. Like I was saying, it ain't no Holiday Inn..."

"Oh, no, that's fine, y'all," boomed Meg. She seemed to have developed a Texas drawl. "Jes' need a place to sleep."

"The beds are clean, I think, or least they were," he muttered. "And there's HBO and cable, but I ain't got no more remote controls, you know, I bought a dozen of them and they were gone in a week."

He led us outside, walking barefoot over the locusts. He was wearing nothing but cutoff sweat pants that hung so low that...well, never mind.

"You two married?" he asked.

"Yep," said Meg.

He gave her a look.

"How come you ain't got no rings?"

"Lost 'em down the garbage disposal," she said.

"Damn! Too bad my friend wasn't there. He can get *anything* out of a garbage disposal." He fumbled about for a key. "Both rings went down the garbage disposal?"

"His went down the toilet," she said.

"Shee-it, don't you lose nothing down the toilets here," he muttered, giving up on the key and kicking the door open. "Don't want nothing stuck in no toilet. None of that. There you go. Like I said, it ain't nothing fancy, no..."

"Holiday Inn," I finished for him. "Uh, the door doesn't have a lock?"

"I guess not." There was a caved-in section near the knob where somebody had apparently kicked it in. "Jes' prop a chair up against the door and you'll be all right."

Dark fake wooden panels, two beds, a TV chained to the wall. But the sheets were clean. We lay down and worshiped the air conditioner. Meg watched a paranoid thriller with John Travolta. I fiddled with my computer and read a posting by someone apparently in the last stages of an overdose.

"Water joe [caffeinated water], good stuff. I use it to make espresso and melt a Vivarin in it instead of a sugar cube or lemon peel and it really goes down smooth but a few minutes later my back starts aching and I have to pee really bad is this normal or what I've never tried snorting Vivarin because it would probably burn and muck up my nose...where did I put that darn Jolt Cola...my dog keeps licking my leg..."

It went on for another period-free six pages. Typical cyber-caffeinated babble. It made me too twitchy to sleep, so we headed out for a beer at the nearby Red Dog Saloon. The place was deserted except for a middle-aged woman and a few dirty-looking guys in trucker caps muttering racial epithets. We opted for Budweisers (like there was a choice) and listened to the lady complain to the bartender about her housing predicament.

"Yep," she was saying. "My husband really wants to move out of my parents' trailer, only he won't go until he finds a spot with good fishing."

"I can understand that," said the bartender. "Gotta find the right neighborhood."

"And a' course the kids would like it too."

Kids? She lived in a trailer with her parents, husband, and kids, plural? Meg and I finished our beers. This was just too depressing, especially when you considered that, despite her extended family, the woman was sitting alone in the Red Dog Saloon at midnight. As we left, the bartender warned us not to talk to the fellows in the parking lot. It was the white supremacists from inside, no doubt conducting a little methadrine deal.

"Where y'all hurryin' off to?" one called out as we approached our car. "We're good company here at the Red Dog. Why don't y'all come back in for a while?"

We muttered something about driving all day, omitting to mention that we'd carelessly allowed our Aryan Nation memberships to expire.

"What hotel y'all staying at?"

I thought about our room with a door that didn't lock.

"Uh, the White Plaza," I lied.

"Don't know that one. Say, you're welcome to stay at me and my friend's place." He pointed down the lightless road. "Just down a way."

We made vague no-thank-you noises. He came a little closer. His friend got out of his truck.

"Maybe next time," I jumped into the car. "Y'all have a nice night."

"All right then," he said. "Maybe we'll all run into you again."

"He seemed sweet," said Meg, as we drove back to the hotel. "Do you think he could be my new boyfriend?"

THE FACT THAT AMERICA LEARNED TO MAKE DECENT COFFEE ON the heels of its first major military defeat makes wonderful fodder for the coffeecentric history of civilization (not to mention the Joffe Coffee Theory of Expansionism). Unfortunately, it is probably best understood as part of the 60s rebellion against overprocessed food. Think whole wheat bread = whole bean coffee. So it's no surprise that the specialty coffee movement was born in the counterculture capital of Berkeley, California, when a gentleman named Alfred Peet opened Peet's Tea and Coffee. They specialized in fresh dark roast coffee and were so successful that his partners soon opened their own places, like Boston's Coffee Connection, Florida's Barney's, and, of course, Seattle's Starbucks, giving birth to an industry now worth about six billion dollars annually.

At the top of this food chain is the ubiquitous Starbucks. It has become quite fashionable to rag on the little mermaid (that's the lady in their logo; Starbucks is the first mate in Moby Dick). There are entire Web sites devoted to lambasting the company. But I'm going to have to differ. Sure, they're a megacorporation destroying hundreds of mom-and-pop cafés. But that's just something large corporations do. The important thing is that they serve fine coffee. Their baristas are generally first-rate. I say this with a grimace—it goes against every grain in my body—but if I'd seen a Starbucks in the wastelands of Oklahoma my joy would have been equal to that of al-Shadhili's when Allah first revealed to him the secret of the coffee bean a thousand years ago. As far as our quest was concerned, however, Starbucks was persona non grata, because it can no more make a great cup of American coffee than Verdi can write rhythm and blues. It operates entirely within an Italian esthetic of espressos and cappuccinos, the antithesis of the indigenous American brewing technique best described as stewing. This tragedy can largely be traced back to the intensely popular *White House Cookbook*, a collection of presidential recipes whose 1887 introduction boasts that it "represents the progress and present perfection of the culinary art."

Among the hundreds of dishes, including squirrel soup, is the single most influential coffee recipe in the history of the United States.

BOILED COFFEE

One coffee cup full of ground coffee, stirred with one egg and part of the shell, adding a half cup of cold water. Put in the coffee boiler and pour onto it a quart of boiling water. As it rises and begins to boil, stir it down with a silver spoon or fork. Boil hard for 10 or 12 minutes. Remove from the fire and pour out a cupful of coffee then pour back into the coffeepot. Keep hot, but not boiling, for another five minutes. Send to the table HOT."

This is nothing less than the atomic bomb of coffee brewing. There is no bean in the world, nay, not the finest Jamaican Blue Mountain, nor the most resonant of the Aged Sumatras, that can retain its exotic overtones when subjected to such abuse. It can, however, when done properly, produce a furry cup, said to be emblematic of the Texas Panhandle through which we were now cruising.

"You'll find it there, boys. Don't you worry. That's Golden Urn country. If you're near Pflugerville, try Dot's Café," wrote ryannon@worldnet.net as we crossed the Oklahoma-Texas border. "I know what you mean, though. Truck stops just don't do coffee the way they used to."

I still don't know where the hell Pflugerville is, because we were determined to stay on the Route 66 highway all the way to LA. Only problem was, we couldn't find it on the map. It was only when we were deep in the Panhandle, driving on the six-lane I-40, that we noticed a lonely little two-lane blacktop running alongside, appearing and disappearing, like a kid brother who wants to play with the big boys. It was Route 66, removed from the maps by the feds when they put in I-40, but still there. Fifty years back it was the route followed by thousands of Americans fleeing West, and its little towns—Amarillo, McLean, Jericho, Conway—were mini-Meccas where travelers refueled on petroleum and coffee. Today nothing but a thousand mile long ghost town littered with abandoned gas stations and boarded-up coffeeshops.

It was like this all Saturday. Sunday morning we saw a weathered blue billboard peeking over the edge of a boarded-up hotel. Adrien's Coffeeshop. We pulled off the main road to see if anybody was home and ran into a handpainted sign that read "Welcome to Adrien! You Are Now Exactly Midway Between Chicago and Los Angeles on the Old Route 66! Come on in!"

We did. The place was decorated with cow skulls and JESUS LOVES YOU license plates. The bathrooms had screen doors on them. We ordered a cup. It proved to be the first all-American joe we'd found—black, tarry, and powerful, rich with half-and-half, cascading in waves from the waitress's Pyrex coffeepot and into our mugs, breaking over us, washing through our veins like rocket fuel. It was awful and terrifying and beyond compare.

"Actually, this coffee isn't that bad," I said, once my tongue's trembling had come under control.

"It's the best," said Meg.

Church services had just ended, and the locals were coming in, all dolled up in flowered dresses and ten-gallon hats. Even the preachers were there, including an older fellow with immaculate silver hair and his fat-faced son of about twenty, both wearing three-piece polyesters and flashing pearly white shit-eaters. Would have thought they were running for president, the way those two carried on. Our sweet-faced waitresses made us happy with T-bones and handcut fries. We finished with the finest blackberry cobbler I've ever eaten, fresh from the oven, crowned with a dollop of creamy synthetic vanilla ice cream. Manna.

"This is the greatest pie I've ever had in my life," said Meg. We ordered another serving. "This is the greatest place, don't you think?"

I thought that was laying it on a little strong. "It's not bad," I agreed.

"This is it, right?" Meg was begging. "No more research, please?"

Meg wasn't looking too good. We'd been consuming about twelve cups of Black Death a day, in addition to large amounts of ephedrine, a legal speed popular with truck drivers. We didn't know it then, but the FDA had recently made caffeine-ephedrine "cocktails" illegal because they produced a number of symptoms we were both experiencing, such as laughing spasms alternating with intense paranoia and depression.[1] I was even getting the twitching-eyeball syndrome common among caffeine-crazy crews on nuclear submarines. I noticed that Meg's brightly glazed, blue eyeballs seemed about to pop out of her head.

"Okay," I said. "This is the best cup."

"You mean the worst, right?"

"It's the best of the worst," I said. "And that'll have to be

[1] Our old friend from Yemen, *qat*, is closely related to ephedrine. Both contain the same active chemical and cause similar effects. There's also a form of meta-*qat*, called Jeff, Mulva, or Cat, gaining a following in America's underground drug market.

good enough."

After Adrien, we understood Texas. The spineless Christian gospel coming out of our radio was supposed to sound the way our air conditioner felt. It was all about smooth living, tight jeans, and the love of the Lord Jesus H. Christ. A-merica, A-men. I was so spaced out I came within inches of sideswiping a station wagon full of kids. But they weren't angry, they were Texan, and showered us with little paw-paws of Christian love as they pulled up alongside. Thank you, sir, said their weird little grins, for almost sending us to Our Savior.

"I could see living here," Meg muttered over and over. "I could live here the rest of my life. I think I just love Texas. Maybe I was a cowgirl in another life."

I told her how on fine nights the cowboys parked their pickups in a circle, turned on their headlights, and, with every radio tuned to the same station, held dances in the middle of the prairie.

I thought Meg was going to cry.

"Can you just drop me off at the next town?" she said.

From Adrien we headed north toward Taos, New Mexico. The flatlands shriveled into red-rock cliffs. The air grew drier. But once the Adrien euphoria was gone, we knew we could be anywhere. Every place had the same restaurants, the same buildings; even the same food, all cooked on the other side of the continent, flash-frozen, shipped, and then reheated until any surviving flavor was sent screaming to oblivion. It's the American way: buy a piece of land in the middle of nothing, divide it into cubicles, then clean it until it smells like nothing, cool it til it feels like nothing, and paint it the color of nothing. When you've driven the local businesses out, start raising the rent. None of it was real. If I pushed on the accelerator, the view out the window changed. If I pushed a computer keyboard button, the computer screen did likewise, with more postings pouring in every minute.

"Caffeine allows me to get closer to my god," came on as we hit Arizona. "But now his voice is fading away. I have constantly increased the strength but now I'm putting so much in, the powder has trouble dissolving...I need pure caffeine...PLEASE HELP ME"

It seemed to me, driving through the desolate Navajo reservation in Arizona, that each age had used the bean according to its understanding of reality. The early coffee cults of Ethiopia and the Middle East saw the drug as a doorway to the mind of God. The secular humanists of eighteenth-century Europe used it as a tool to create a reasoned society. We citizens of the brave new world, who worship efficiency and speed, are just turning it into a high, another way to go a little faster, get there a bit quicker, and feel a little better. To hell with the consequences.

The rest of the trip is a blur. I remember Meg and me being the only customers in a cavernous Cracker Coffeeshop near Flagstaff at three in the morning, laughing so uncontrollably that the waitress refused to refill our cups. I remember the rancid coffee at the Circus Circus All-You-Can-Eat Breakfast Buffet in Vegas, and the lady at the next table weeping as she tallied all the money she had lost; the streets full of the ugly, the stupid, and the greedy and Larry, the blackjack dealer from Laos. And always more ephedrine and more coffee and more gin and Meg always laughing in the next seat, singing out of tune, but laughing, laughing so hard she's shaking with the strain. Only now she's in the driver's seat and there are hundreds of cars swirling around us. We're in the middle of some monster-size merger on the freeway into downtown Los Angeles—we'd made it to the West Coast!—but Meg can't stop laughing, and it's so bad she can't steer anymore, she's slowing down to a dead stop in the middle of the freeway while thousands of leather-faced L.A.

commuters swirl around us like locusts, screaming and furious, shaking their fists and honking—how dare you slow down! Don't ever slow down! Go, go, go! But Meg is not going anywhere; she's gone, gone, gone, tears of laughter rolling down her face, lips curled back in a grin like an angry dog.

Acknowledgments

Thanks, *danke*, *merci*, and *asante sana* to the following. To my wife (if she'll have me), Nina J. To Tanya La Taz (for refusing to marry me). To my brother Troy and his wife Paula, for lodging me for three months, and Tom Yee of SF for not evicting me when he could have. Gratitude to my editor Juri Jurjevics at Soho for his pithy editorial observations (is *ugh*! really a proofreading symbol?) and my agent Felicia Eth for perseverance beyond the call of duty. Kisses to Jeff for all those C's. To Annabel Bentley for her accommodating ways. Special thanks to Abera of Harrar, and a variety of Yemeni men whose names I could never pronounce, and of course Yangi for such outstanding con skills. To Josef Joffe for his insightful speculations. Thanks to the few million that made the trip so annoying, and of course the legions of cyber denizens on Alt.caffeine, coffee, H-France, etc., whose generous supply of information and misinformation could keep anybody mystified for centuries.

Special thanks to the Johann Jacobs Museum in Zurich, Switzerland; the Bramah Tea and Coffee Museum in London; the archives of Catherine Cotelle; the British Museum, Asian Wing; the French National Library; the New York Research Library; the libraries of the Universities of California, Berkeley and Los Angeles; the Municipal Library of Addis Ababa; the Library of the University of Addis Ababa; the unnamed library in Sana'a, Yemen; London's Guildhall Library; Vienna's National Library; the municipal libraries of San Francisco and Los Angeles, and probably a few others.